Elements of
Parliamentary Debate

Elements of Parliamentary Debate

A Guide to Public Argument

Trischa Goodnow Knapp
Oregon State University

Lawrence A. Galizio
Portland Community College

LONGMAN

An imprint of Addison Wesley Longman, Inc.

New York • Reading, Massachusetts • Menlo Park, California • Harlow, England
Don Mills, Ontario • Sydney • Mexico City • Madrid • Amsterdam

Acquisitions Editor: Donna Erickson
Marketing Manager: John Holdcroft
Project Manager: Ellen MacElree
Design Manager: Wendy Fredericks
Cover Designer: Kay Petronio
Prepress Services Supervisor: Valerie A. Vargas
Print Buyer: Denise Sandler
Electronic Page Makeup: David Munger/DTC

The Elements of Parliamentary Debate: A Guide to Public Argument by
Trischa Goodnow Knapp and Lawrence A. Galizio

Please visit our Web site at http://longman.awl.com

ISBN 0-321-02470-2

In memory of Vincent A. Galizio,
a curmudgeon with a sense of humor
who taught me to question authority
and think outside the box

and

To James E. (Jimmy) Goodnow II
and in memory of Al Formica,
both taught me early on that arguing isn't about winning;
it's about seeing the world from a variety of perspectives

Contents

Contents

Preface

Given the need to develop skills in public argument, *Elements of Parliamentary Debate: A Guide to Public Argument* was born of necessity. Although the practice of competitive parliamentary debate has witnessed exponential growth in colleges and universities throughout North America and now boasts the largest parliamentary debating organization in the world (the National Parliamentary Debate Association), we have found no text available for educators and competitors participating in North America's adaptation of this European-inspired format for debate. We believe that parliamentary debate is a useful and unexplored exercise for teaching argumentation skills in the classroom. Yet again, no text has been available to aid teachers in using this method.

As directors of forensics and educators in the field of speech communication, we have had the opportunity to witness firsthand the precipitous growth of parliamentary debate throughout the United States. The recent expansion has been especially significant in both the midwestern and western regions of the United States where it has literally transformed the collegiate forensics landscape. We believe this transformation should also make its way into the argumentation classroom. Since public argument often relies on extemporaneous thinking and speaking, parliamentary debate offers a constructive platform for developing these skills.

At the same time, as educators, we have also struggled with the largely avoidable misunderstandings, disagreements, and misinformation about parliamentary debate among coaches and competitors alike. Educators and competitors eager for instruction in this debating format have thus far struggled without the assistance of the accumulated information and theory of those more familiar with the activity. Consequently, participants have relied on hearsay and the occasional handout covering the "how-tos" and "what-ifs" for their instruction. *Elements of Parliamentary Debate* seeks to answer this need.

Furthermore, as educators teaching courses in argumentation, we have come to recognize the utility of parliamentary debate as a laboratory and practicum for argumentation theory. In-class debates among students in college argumentation courses have both strengthened students' comprehension of argumentation theory and popularized the course among undergraduates eager for active and participatory learning. In-class parliamentary debates unfailingly stimulate active discussion of logical fallacies, refutation, and overall strategic argumentation. We strongly encourage teachers of the undergraduate argumentation course to familiarize themselves with parliamentary debate and experiment with it as a supplement to lecture and discussion.

Recognizing that forensics and argumentation educators have a multiplicity of coaching and teaching styles, along with divergent perspectives concerning theory, strategy, and pedagogy for debating and argumentation, we offer this guide as a reference for educators and students interested in or now practicing parliamentary debate. We hope that this collection of easily accessible material on the basics of parliamentary debate will provide all participants with a reliable yet flexible guide to accompany their journey toward mastery of this dynamic format for debate.

FEATURES OF ELEMENTS OF PARLIAMENTARY DEBATE

Coverage of the debate process. The topics in *Elements of Parliamentary Debate* are arranged to aid study and permit easy reference for students and instructors. The book is arranged to reflect how we view the parliamentary debate process, beginning with the areas that students must understand before they ever engage in a parliamentary debate, namely, the resolution, the nature of argument, fallacies and research. We then consider the debating process, including a description of the goals of both sides in the debate, as well as the purpose of each of the speeches. Finally, we encounter the postdebate process, understanding the outcomes of debates and steps for the advanced debater.

Flexible organization. Each of the chapters in *Elements of Parliamentary Debate* stands by itself; readers need consult only those parts of the book covering the aspects of debating with which they need further help. If an instructor would prefer to spend more time on lectures and discussion of the material, sections of the book may be assigned to the entire class.

Easy-to-understand explanations. Parliamentary debate preparation, case construction, resolutional analysis, refutation, argumentation, delivery, and adjudication are detailed in clear, concise language.

Additional resources. Appendices including sample ballots, flow sheets, and additional research areas are included to enable readers to clarify misunderstandings and analyze what an actual debate round is like.

Finally, we must voice one caveat regarding the use of this book. This guide is not intended to replace texts that undertake thorough discussions of argumentation theory. Rather, this book is intended to complement those texts, providing a practical guide to using argumentation theory in the parliamentary debate format. For more complete discussions of argumentation theory, we suggest readers consult standard texts such as Richard Rieke and Malcolm Sillars's *Argumentation and Critical Decision Making.*

Videotaped copies of two parliamentary debate rounds are available at an additional cost through the Oregon State University forensics program. For more information call (541) 737-5391.

ACKNOWLEDGMENTS

Madame Speaker, Members of the Parliament, we would like to take this opportunity to thank those who, knowingly or unknowingly, contributed to the construction of this text. First, thanks to Deirdre Cavanaugh, our original editor at Longman and her colleagues Peter Harris and Kwon Chong. Thanks also to Donna Erickson—this book would not have been completed without her help. We gratefully acknowledge the suggestions and support of the reviewers of this book: Nick Backus, *Washburn University;* Robert Branham, *Bates College;* Douglas Fraleigh, *California State University—Fresno;* Rene Gernant, *Concordia College;* Jeffrey Dale Hobbs, *Abilene Christian University;* Beverly M. Kelley, *California Lutheran University;* Duane Pifer, *Louisiana Tech University;* C. Thomas Preston Jr., *University of Missouri, St. Louis;* and Tammy Duvanel Unruh, *Bethel College.*

Our accumulated knowledge and understanding of parliamentary debate can be blamed on our colleagues in the National Parliamentary Debate Association, especially the Johnsons: James "Al" and Steven L. "Topic Area" (no, we don't even mention topic areas in this book). Equally important are the hundreds of students who have endured our adjudication and have constantly reminded us of the value of public argument and forensics competition. To our own teams—past, present, and future—thanks for suffering through vans, planes, and automobiles and the willing suspension of disbelief that Motel 6 is a five-star hotel and McDonald's is haute cuisine.

We wish to acknowledge the Oregon State University Center for the Humanities for providing support to Trischa for the writing of this text.

Finally, thanks to the right honorable Lee Rianda, who was especially invaluable in proofreading the manuscript. And biggest thanks of all to Loril Chandler, who dealt with our inadequacies and eccentricities while she prepared the layout for this text.

Introduction

What Is Parliamentary Debate?

Whenever tragedy strikes at the heart of America, whether natural disaster, unexplainable violence, or unexpected loss, we search for answers. In the aftermath of these tragedies, the public conversations that help to mitigate the anger, frustration, and guilt for the people of the communities directly affected are echoed nationally as Americans grapple with the sense of helplessness.

Conversations designed to deal with these feelings are inevitable and necessary in a democratic society for both the individual and the community at large. Individuals, who come to terms with events in their own time, can seek support from others in the community and fulfill the need to act, even if it is just having their voice heard. Town meetings, letters to the editor, call-in radio shows, and Internet chat rooms are examples of venues where the public dialogue continues. These public discussions can then lead to action for positive change.

Within these discussions we discover the need for skills in public argumentation and debate. From the grieving mother seeking accountability to the congressional representative crafting legislation, the ability to persuade is paramount. The cultivation of persuasion and argumentative skills is the *raison d'être* of academic debate. The competitive format that most resembles these public discussions is parliamentary debate.

Academic debate differs from the everyday debate you engage in with friends most noticeably in its structured format. Unlike the free flow and often chaotic nature of debates with friends, academic debate requires that participants take turns and adhere to previously specified time limits and guidelines. Though our goal in this book is to cover the format of one type of debate, all academic debate formats begin with a certain area of controversy. Parliamentary debate is a fun, engaging debate style requiring students to exhibit knowledge of a broad cross section of ideas while displaying exemplary rhetorical skills. Parliamentary debate requires students to use and analyze language in ways that are new and exciting. In addition, understanding how the terminology of parliamentary debate is used enables students to appreciate the unique spirit of this debate format.

We believe that parliamentary debate should not be relegated to use only in extracurricular activities. Rather, parliamentary debate can be used in the argumentation class as well. Parliamentary debate is a user-friendly debate format, allowing students to utilize the knowledge they already possess and thus providing an interactive forum for developing and practicing argumentative skills. This handbook is designed to introduce both teachers and students to a readily approachable debate format.

THE NATURE OF PARLIAMENTARY DEBATE

Prepared debate formats, such as those usually practiced in the argumentation classroom and in many competitive debate formats, ask students to acquire an in-depth, specialized knowledge of a specific topic area. Students can and often do spend twenty hours a week or more doing research into the topic area. Students take this knowledge and develop cases, learning argumentation skills in the process.

Parliamentary debate, on the other hand, asks students to draw from their own knowledge to develop cases and to refute the case of the opposing team. Parliamentary debate offers a new *resolution* or topic for each debate. Students then have fifteen minutes to prepare their cases. The following discussion in this introduction concerns the conventions of parliamentary debate focusing on form rather than content since the majority of this handbook is devoted to the latter topic.

Those familiar with C-SPAN's coverage of the Prime Minister's Question Time from Britain's House of Parliament will no doubt recognize some of the language in parliamentary debate since this format is based on the British Parliament. For debaters, the ramifications of this model extend far beyond protocol and the labels for participants. The influence of this model pervades the entire structure and character of parliamentary debating. Consequently, some of the conventions of that form remain as a nod to the British tradition. The first of these conventions is the naming of the teams, *Government* and *Opposition*. The Government's burden is to affirm the resolution while the Opposition attempts to negate the resolution. The teams are composed of two competitors each; the Prime Minister and Member of Government compose the Government team, and the Leader of the Opposition and the Member of the Opposition compose the Opposition team.

Both teams are given the resolution at the same time and then are given fifteen minutes to prepare their cases. Resolutions are stated from the perspective of *the House*: *This House believes* or *This House would*. Resolutions often focus on questions of *fact*, *value*, or *policy*; these can be considered directions for the debate. Topics are generally of two types: *straight* or *abstract*. Straight resolutions define a specific topic for debate: *This House believes the public right to know does not extend to court cases; This House would give racists a platform*. Abstract resolutions are broad topics that allow the Government team to link the resolution to an infinite number of issues. Examples of abstract resolutions include *This House believes might makes right; This House would explode the canon*.

After the resolution is announced, the teams prepare for fifteen minutes outside the debating chambers.

Once the preparation time is over and the debate begins, the speaking times are divided as follows:

Prime Minister constructive	7 minutes
Leader of Opposition constructive	8 minutes
Member of Government constructive	8 minutes
Member of Opposition constructive	8 minutes
Leader of Opposition rebuttal	4 minutes
Prime Minister rebuttal	5 minutes

Notice that there is no designated cross-examination period. Instead, *points of information* and *points of order* are available to the speakers. After the first minute and before the last minute of all constructive speeches, the opposing team may offer points of information to the speaker who holds the floor. The purpose of these statements or questions is to clarify a point the speaker is making, advance a point for the opposing team, or highlight a weakness in the other team's case. Points of information foster an interactive style of debate since the opposing team can interrupt the speaker at an appropriate and often strategic time. Conversely, the speaker can refuse to take the point of information. In this way, the speaker holding the floor can maintain control of the allotted speaking time. This interactive format often produces lively, passionate debates.

Points of order are directed to the judge. They are most often used during the rebuttal period to object to a new argument in rebuttal or if the opposing team is misconstruing an argument that the opposing team proposed. The judge must make an immediate ruling on the point of order. No discussion can occur, and the judge does not justify the decision. Since there is only one rebuttal per side, this enables both teams the opportunity to point out unfair strategies used by the opposing team during these speeches.

The actual content of the debate produces two distinctions unique to parliamentary debate. The first is the prohibition of carded evidence or written materials in the debating chambers. Carded evidence is usually evidence from an authority that is read word for word in the round. Debaters using prepared materials provide the source of the information as well as a full citation within the context of their speeches. Parliamentary debaters rely on the various forms of evidence, namely, examples, common knowledge, statistics, analogies, and even authority. Resolutions are written so as to fall within the realm of common knowledge. Consequently, a well-read student will have little problem finding examples, analogies, statistics, or authority to support contentions without citing carded evidence in the round.

The parliamentary debater will research a wide range of topics rather than one specific topic. Preparation is thus different from researching one area. Students who choose to engage in parliamentary debate will read contemporary news sources in addition to reading the basic works of philosophy, politics, and literature. As a result, students use in the debate information that they already know or information that they learn in classes.

The successful parliamentary debater offers a *claim* that warrants support. As anyone who has conversed with a friend about the best restaurant in any given city knows, *evidence* supporting claims takes a variety of forms, including the act of *reasoning* from premises to claim. Support for claims goes well beyond the appeal to authority. This text will visit the question of types of evidence useful in parliamentary debate.

Another distinguishing characteristic of parliamentary debate is the use of *time/space cases*, which remain a controversial tactic at the time of this writing. Time/space cases can be defined as cases where both judges and competitors are removed to a different time and place. Consequently, all facts and judgments must be of that time period. Any information that would be unknown to people in that setting is unacceptable. This approach to a motion requires a clear understanding of its burdens from the standpoint of both the debaters and the adjudicators. This approach is covered in Chapter 23: Time/Space Cases.

SPECIFIC BENEFITS OF PARLIAMENTARY DEBATE

Parliamentary debate has many unique aspects that foster specific skills and benefits for the participant. Parliamentary debate creates opportunities to improve extemporaneous thinking and argument construction, broad-based research skills and knowledge, and the important faculty of memory.

Extemporaneous Thinking

Quite often we find ourselves in situations wherein we must construct arguments "on our feet" or on the spur of the moment. Parliamentary debate's format necessitates this type of extemporaneous argumentation. Although preparation and research certainly take place prior to each debating exercise, ignorance of the specific motions to be considered in each round forces debaters to construct cases and arguments quickly. The cognitive skills used in parliamentary debate translate into an ability to rapidly process, analyze, and discuss complex issues and information. If you think about it, most arguments in which you engage are usually spur-of-the-moment, forcing you to draw on the knowledge that you have accumulated through everyday living. Parliamentary debate allows you to hone argumentation skills that you use in most of your relationships, both private and public.

Broad-Based Research Skills

The tension among educators touting the benefits of a broad-based liberal arts education versus those promoting specialized knowledge remains prominent. Of course, these two ideals are not mutually exclusive.

Since parliamentary debaters do not know beforehand which issues they will be debating, the successful competitor will strive to become conversant on a wide variety of issues and controversies. Familiarities with social and political philosophers, world history, and contemporary issues, along with argumentation and debate theory, are vital to one's success. Parliamentary debate rewards a broad-based liberal arts education and motivates students toward such knowledge.

In addition, students learning parliamentary debate in the argumentation classroom can focus on argumentation skills rather than on accumulating knowledge of a specific topic. With all the constraints that are placed on students in these times, it helps to know that what you're focusing on in a class is argumentation rather than knowing everything there is to know about a topic in six weeks or less. Rather, parliamentary debate allows students to understand how to use the knowledge they already possess to its fullest potential.

Memory: The Rediscovered Canon

In an age when rapid and easy access, retrieval, and storage of information are unprecedented, the attention given to memory has diminished. Nevertheless, the successful extemporaneous communicator has at his or her immediate disposal a wealth of information and knowledge. Likewise, parliamentary debate revives the "lost canon" by forcing debaters to rely on their immediate knowledge base for supporting material for their claims. The fifteen-minute preparation time, together with the prohibition of published materials during the debate, rewards the well-informed student. In turn, the well-informed student can use these skills to become a productive member of society.

CONCLUSION

Parliamentary debate is a user-friendly form of argumentation that allows participants at all levels to come to terms with argumentation and to advance to the upper levels of debate more quickly. Al Johnson, director of forensics at Colorado College and one of the founders of the National Parliamentary Debate Association, writes that parliamentary debate provides "an avenue for inexperienced students and students who normally do only individual events" to practice argumentation (4). Parliamentary debate encourages a return to the fundamentals of argumentation and presentation that can offer advantages to students who pursue the parliamentary opportunity.

Part I

Elements of Debate

Chapter One

Resolutions

Key Concepts

Abstract resolutions—propositions that define the
   relationship among the terms but not necessarily the
   specific issue to be debated

Issues—significant questions inherent to the controversy

Proposition—a statement that suggests the topic to be
   debated [also known as a *motion, resolution* or *topic*]

Resolutions of fact—propositions that ask the debaters to
   prove that a particular claim is more true than false

Resolutions of policy—propositions that ask the debaters to
   develop a plan to solve a particular problem

Resolutions of value—propositions that ask debaters to prove
   that one value is more important than others in a
   particular context

Straight resolutions—propositions in which the subject to be
   debated is clearly defined

Almost everyone is familiar with the term *debate* and the general idea of debating. We debate the merits of a film or the prospect of working overtime versus going out with friends. We debate serious issues such as whether or not military action appears justified or what we might do to narrow the gap between the rich and the poor. Sometimes our debates revolve around less significant issues such as whether *Titanic* was a great film or a great spectacle.

Regardless of the subject or its relative importance, we understand and frequently engage in debate. That is, we make competing claims and discuss the issues we believe are relevant to a larger controversy. For example, your friend claims surfing takes more skill than snowboarding, and you try to convince her the opposite is true. In parliamentary debate, each debate centers around a new topic or **proposition**. A proposition is the specific issue that is the subject of the debate and usually offers an agent and an action. So the proposition will suggest *who* (agent) should do *what* (action). The term *proposition* is a general concept that applies to a variety of different forms of expressing whatever is to be debated. Propositions might also be referred to as *motions, resolutions,* or *topics.*

For example, in most business meetings, propositions are phrased as motions: *I move that we renegotiate the contract with the firm.* In most formats of academic debate and public argument, propositions are phrased as resolutions: *Be it resolved that advertising degrades the quality of life in the United States.* Commissions or boards of inquiry are often responsible for addressing questions: *Does concentrated ownership of mass media in the United States represent a threat to representative democracy?* In like manner, in legislatures and often in parliamentary debate, propositions may be phrased as bills or motions: *We hereby move that the street formerly known as Main will henceforth be known as César Chávez Boulevard.* In a house of parliament, or sometimes in parliamentary debate, propositions are phrased as motions: *This House supports public health over the right to bear arms.* The term *House* refers to the legislative body of the house of parliament. In academic parliamentary debate, most propositions are phrased as motions employing the term *House.*

Our sample propositions raise a host of issues that may or may not be addressed within the debate. **Issues** can be defined as significant questions inherent to the controversy. For example, take the controversial subject area of drug testing in the workplace. Through examination of the subject area, many important issues might be raised:

- What is the definition of "drug"?
- What procedures does the test require?
- What is the justification for the test?
- How much will it cost?
- Is the practice constitutional?
- What are the psychological effects on the tested population?
- Does testing violate the presumption of innocence?

These questions touch on just a few of the issues people might address in a debate on drug testing. Such a controversy gives rise to a multiplicity of issues. This suggests one of the primary reasons for propositions for debate: Propositions endeavor to clarify the focus of the debate by establishing the issues that are in dispute.

Quite often in our debates with friends, we have insufficient understandings of the claims that are made and what exactly our dispute is about. Although you might believe you are struggling over what color to paint the house, the real issue for your roommate might be who will do the bulk of the work. Debate propositions or resolutions help to reduce misunderstandings to the actual focus of the debate.

In addition, this clarification also serves to create a distinct clash of positions. Debaters arguing a resolution should easily recognize their respective interest in the controversy. Propositions help demarcate the dispute.

Finally, propositions give participants in the debate an idea as to the significance of affirming or rejecting the statement. The immediate result of affirming the motion to change the name of Main Street to César Chávez Boulevard would be quite clear. In contrast, debates without a clear proposition might result in misunderstandings of the significance of the dispute. An example of an unclear proposition might be "Pink is better than green." Without a context, this topic has little significance.

In addition, the mode and type of resolution may be different with every debate. Therefore, a fundamental understanding of the modes and types of resolutions is essential to parliamentary debate. In the following pages, we will outline the modes of resolutions (abstract or straight) and the types of resolutions (fact, value, or policy).

MODES OF RESOLUTIONS

Resolutions can be either straight or abstract. **Straight resolutions** dictate a relatively specific topic area. These areas most often concern matters in the public domain. Examples include *This House believes U.S. domestic policy should be guided by the principle of diversity; This House believes efforts to protect the public's right to know have gone too far; This House should slow progress on the information superhighway.*

Abstract topics, by contrast, do not necessarily delineate any specific issue. **Abstract resolutions** show a clear relationship between the terms in the topic without clearly defining the issue that must be debated. These resolutions are open to any reasonable interpretation by the Government team. Abstract resolutions are often derived from famous, and sometimes infamous, quotations. Examples include *This House believes someday my prince will come, someday I'll find the one; This House believes a rose by any other name would smell as sweet; This House believes life is like a box of chocolates—you never know what you're gonna get; This House would open its doors.*

In addition, some resolutions may be philosophical, requiring debaters to argue about abstract concepts. Philosophical resolutions are classified as abstract because many Government teams choose to make the resolution debatable by linking the relationship of terms in the resolution to more concrete ideas in the real world. An example of a philosophical resolution would be *This House believes the only constant is change.*

Both the Government and Opposition teams must determine what is a reasonable interpretation of the resolution. Perhaps the most important standard for determining if the interpretation is reasonable is to decide if the interpretation provides debatable ground for both the Government and the Opposition. The Government clearly has the advantage in interpreting since the Government need only determine the one reasonable interpretation it wishes to defend. The Opposition must determine the bounds of reasonableness for the particular resolution in question. We'll discuss these issues at greater length in the chapters devoted to developing cases and preparation time.

Whether the resolution is straight or abstract, the Government team must succinctly state the exact resolution that it hopes to uphold in the round. For example, if the resolution is the *someday my prince will come* topic from above, the Government might choose to advocate selecting Candidate X for president. The Government would need to state, "In this round, we will define *prince* as Candidate X. The idea of *my prince will come* means that Candidate X is the best person for the presidency." In this way, the Opposition is clear as to exactly what it must oppose. We will delve more into these ideas in the chapter on defining terms.

TYPES OF RESOLUTIONS

Interpreting the resolution is unwieldy at best, frustratingly impossible at worst. In prepared debate formats, teams have weeks and even months to consider the pros and cons of all possible interpretations. Parliamentary debaters have a mere fifteen minutes to develop a case. To aid in the process, teams can turn to three more specific areas of interpretation. Resolutions may be of fact, value, or policy.

Resolutions of fact ask the question whether a condition is more true than not. An example of a factual resolution is *This House believes that the Brady Law has been ineffective in curbing gun violence.* Clearly, both sides in the debate have distinctive ground to cover; the Brady Law has either helped or not helped. Neither side in a factual debate should attempt to argue a known or accepted fact. Given the resolution *This House believes Elvis is dead*, the Government would be arguing a fact. However, to make the round debatable, the Government could argue that the fascination with Elvis has diminished of late. Consequently, the debate would be an argument as to whether the factual claim that Elvis's popularity has dwindled is more true than not.

Resolutions of value offer competing value systems that the opposing teams must resolve through a value hierarchy. In the case of the resolution *This House believes the rights of the accused are more important that the public right to know*, the values of justice and a free press are in competition. The debate then centers on which is more important, or in the case of the Opposition, the claim that the values are at least of equal importance.

Resolutions of policy ask the Government to advocate a specific policy to remedy a specific problem. The resolution *This House should install speed bumps on the information superhighway* asks the Government to propose specific policies to slow down the rate of progress of the information superhighway.

We should note here that the notions of fact, value, and policy can and do overlap. To determine which policy we should adopt, we need a value to guide the policy. Certainly factual claims are required to show the importance of values in action. A good, clean debate will identify the type of resolution, the relationship among facts, values, and policies, and how the resolution can be evaluated. If the Government does not make these issues clear, the Opposition must clarify them through points of information or by asserting these issues in the Leader of Opposition's first speech.

Since we are called on to discuss a variety of issues that encompass the realm of fact, value, and policy in everyday life, parliamentary debate offers the opportunity to practice debating each of these types of propositions. Though each type of resolution asks the teams to prove different things, during prep time both teams should determine the type of resolution that they are debating.

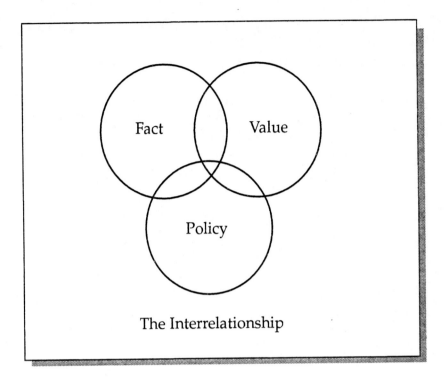

The Interrelationship

Naming the resolution type is a crucial step that teams often overlook. By identifying the type, a team then knows how to proceed in developing its case.

CONCLUSION

The broad nature of the modes and types of resolutions should be a red flag to good parliamentary debaters who are prepared to debate a wide variety of topics. In addition, the best debates are the ones in which the issues are clarified by the debaters. Some teams who think they will trick the Opposition by not defining what they are defending usually end up defeating themselves in the process. Identifying fact, value, or policy will make the debate easier to follow for everyone involved. We will explore further how cases can be built on each of these resolution types in later chapters.

Chapter Two

What Is an Argument?

Key Concepts

Argument—reasoned decision making

Causal reasoning—reasoning that implies that one condition or event is the result of another

Claim—a debatable assertion

Deductive reasoning—reasoning that applies a held conclusion to a specific case

Evidence—data accepted as true that can be used to prove claims

Examples—evidence in the form of specific cases; examples can be categorical, hypothetical, metaphorical, or analogical

Expert testimony—evidence that draws on authority

Inductive reasoning—reasoning that draws a general conclusion by considering specific cases

Parallel case—reasoning that asserts that two cases are similar enough to draw conclusions about one case based on the other case

Reasoning—stated or unstated reasons why a claim should be accepted

Sign reasoning—reasoning that draws conclusions from states that are observable in other states

Statistics—evidence that provides numerical quantification of information

Parliamentary debate provides a laboratory for argumentation. In this chapter, we will examine the basic structure of argumentation and its relationship to the practice of parliamentary debate.

Argument can be defined as the use of evidence and reasoning to support claims. Hollihan and Baaske apply the notion of argument to everyday life. Their definition, "the claims that people make when they are asserting their opinions and supporting their beliefs," illustrates the routine use of argument in our communication (4).

Take, for example, the statement "Franklin D. Roosevelt was the greatest president in the history of the United States because a poll of five hundred prominent historians said so." This is an example of an argument since the reasoning supports the claim. We shall use this example to illustrate an approach to argument based on the work of philosopher Stephen Toulmin.

The popular Toulmin model for argument dissects an argument into distinct parts or elements for analysis and understanding. Although Toulmin divides an argument into six elements, we believe a focus on three primary elements of the argument model represents a more functional initial approach. The three primary components of an argument are:

- Claim or conclusion
- Evidence or data
- Reasoning or warrant

When we engage in argument, we assert a claim and then attempt to prove that the claim is true. In the above example, the person who asserts that claim is attempting to prove that Franklin Roosevelt was the greatest president in the history of the United States. The experts who assert this claim provide evidence to prove the claim. Since so many experts agree with this claim, we can draw the conclusion that it must be correct.

Imagine engaging in an argument with someone who asserts without proving. Does this scenario sound familiar? A friend says that television violence leads to violence among children. You ask her for proof and she replies, "It's common sense." It may be common sense, but that doesn't make it true. Without proof, we cannot accept the claim. The whole of parliamentary debate is dependent on this basic premise of argumentation. The purpose of this chapter, then, is to discuss the very basic elements of an argument.[1]

[1] Our purpose in this chapter is not to delve into the intricacies of argument. In this

CLAIM

The **claim** is the assertion you are hoping to prove. A claim is a statement that requires some proof before it is accepted. The claim is made in the form of a statement: "politicians are not trustworthy." Clearly, such a statement is debatable.

Two problems can occur with the statement of the claim. The first problem occurs when the claim stated is not debatable. If it does not require proof to be accepted then it is an accepted fact, and therefore, not debatable. Suppose I assert that the sky is blue (assuming a cloudless day). Going through the process of proving the claim to be true is generally a waste of time and energy when the principle itself is generally accepted.

A second problem occurs when a claim is mistakenly stated as a question. In this case, a debater might begin an argument by saying, "Are politicians trustworthy?" The speaker is not making an assertion that is provable. Debaters are not in the game to ask questions. Rather, they are in the game to test and prove assertions.

Claims should also be stated in complete sentences. Debaters will sometimes just announce the point of the claim. For example, a student might announce, "problem." Well, what about it? Make sure claims are in complete thoughts and sentences. "Problem" does not make a debatable claim; it is just a word.

EVIDENCE

Here we shall discuss the basic types of **evidence**, or forms of data that provide proof for a claim, of which there are three: examples, statistics, and authority.

Examples come in a variety of forms. Some texts will list each of the forms as a separate type of evidence. **Examples** can be defined as particular cases that are linked to the subject either categorically, hypothetically, metaphorically, or analogically.

Categorical examples are actual cases that are strictly representative of the issue at hand. Suppose the resolution is *AIDS patients are responsible for their plight*. The Opposition might argue that certain medical situations have, in the

---

chapter, we will merely give you the essentials of an argument and how those can be used in a debate. Refer to Reike and Sillars for a more extensive discussion of the theory of argumentation.

past, exposed a person to AIDS due to no action by the individual. The Opposition might cite the case of Ryan White, a teenager who contracted the AIDS virus through a blood transfusion. The example is categorically defined.

Similar to categorical examples, hypothetical examples are fictional cases that are strictly representative of the case at hand. These types of examples are often used when no actual case is readily available. When using hypothetical examples, the fictional account should be as realistic as possible. If we take our example of the AIDS resolution, suppose the Opposition did not know of the Ryan White case. The Opposition could still argue that a patient could contract the AIDS virus unknowingly through a blood transfusion. Hypothetically, the situation could occur. Though no specific case is mentioned, the Opposition assumes a fictitious victim. Some situations may lend themselves to creating a fictitious name, such as Jane Doe. Named or not, without a specific case, the example is fictitious yet still provides support for a claim.

Metaphorical examples will attempt to prove the claim by likening the case at hand to a hypothetical situation that is dissimilar except in effects. Perhaps the most recognizable argument by metaphor is the antidrug public service announcement that shows an egg cooking in a frying pan. The voice-over states, "This is your brain," referring to the egg. As the egg sizzles in the pan, the voice-over continues, "This is your brain on drugs. Any questions?" The commercial equates two dissimilar things—a brain and an egg—and the effect that drugs and heat have on the substances, respectively.

Metaphors are used best when attempting to simplify the explanation of a complex process. Metaphors enable the recipient to grasp the concept through a readily identifiable process such as a frying egg. When using metaphors, debaters must remember to make sure that the metaphor does not oversimplify the problem.

Analogical examples compare like cases so that what is true of one will most likely be true of the other. During the Persian Gulf War, two analogies were used repeatedly as a guide to United States policy in the Gulf: the Munich analogy and the Vietnam analogy. Let us consider each of these analogies and decide its usefulness. The Munich analogy refers to the policy of appeasement that annexed the Czech territory to Germany prior to World War II. The Axis powers reasoned that allowing Hitler to command the Czech territory would appease him and prevent further aggression in Europe on Hitler's part. Unfortunately, Hitler took the policy of appeasement as a weakness and soon began to fight for the rest of Europe.

President Bush likened Iraqi President Saddam Hussein to Hitler to raise the fear that allowing Hussein to retain Kuwait would encourage the Iraqi army to attempt a take over of the Middle East. At first glance, this may seem an appropriate analogy. However, on closer inspection we find that Iraq did not have the military strength to deploy an all-out takeover of the Middle East. Further, Hussein had domestic complications that Hitler did not have. The analogy failed, and Bush shifted to the Vietnam analogy.

President Bush chose to use Vietnam as a negative analogy. In this case, Bush outlined the similarities between Vietnam and the Persian Gulf (limited as they were) to outline a strategy that would lead to the belief that the Gulf War would not be another Vietnam. Bush argued that though both were small countries thrust into war with the great United States, the Persian Gulf War would be a swift, decisive victory. The problem with this analogy was again that the situations were too dissimilar to merit comparison. Vietnam was a country covered in thick jungle, whereas the Gulf War was fought in the desert. Vietnam was in part a civil war, whereas the Gulf War involved one country invading another. The differences were numerous. Analogies such as these are common in parliamentary debate.

Examples are perhaps the most popular evidence form in parliamentary debate. Well-read students have a plethora of examples at their fingertips. Indeed, well-prepared students will have historical, literary, political, and popular examples from which to draw. Examples are useful in illustrating the value paradigms that many parliamentary topics suggest. Topics that suggest policy considerations are also aided by the use of examples. Although preparation time in parliamentary debate does not allow for in-depth development of a Government plan, examples from policies already enacted are often adequate to prove a suggested Government plan.

Statistics

Statistics are the numerical quantification of information. Because carded evidence is prohibited, statistics are used sparingly in parliamentary debate. Statistical use is limited to statistics that are accepted generally as true. For example, that one in every two marriages in the United States ends in divorce is generally accepted. We would also accept the statistic that George Bush had 90 percent approval ratings for his handling of the Gulf War. However, should a debater cite the number of homicides in Los Angeles during 1993, the opposing team has several options: it can ask for clarification in a point of information, refute the information in the claim, or rise to a point of order. The point of order is rarely heard, but it is an acceptable strategy. It is up to the judge's discretion to determine if the information cited is specific evidence.

Expert Testimony

Expert testimony is the reference to an authoritative source on a given subject. First, let us consider standard types of expert testimony. The most common type of expert testimony is a direct quotation from a credible source that retains the spirit of the original context. However, fidelity to this form is virtually impossible in parliamentary debate since direct quotations read from cards are prohibited. Still, this does not prohibit students from relying on expert testimony. It is common for students to use two forms of expert testimony in parliamentary rounds: specific statements and policy ideas.

The first type of expert testimony is famous quotations or commonly known ideas attributable to one person. For example, on a resolution concerning public safety versus the right to privacy, a Government team might cite Supreme Court Justice Oliver Wendell Holmes's famous example that you cannot falsely shout fire in a crowded theater. Since this is considered common knowledge, it is not necessary to cite the specific source. At this point, the example has a life of its own. Consequently, the example does not need the authority of its source to establish the credibility of the evidence. However, in classification, this is still a form of expert testimony.

The second type of expert testimony commonly used in parliamentary debate is from experts in policy. In this case, it is not merely words or ideas that are owned by a person but rather specific policy recommendations. For example, consider a resolution that states that the system of health care in the United States should be reformed. Either team may find itself citing a senator's plan to cut back on Medicare for the elderly. More often than not, teams will cite the source of their plan since similar policies are often floated by other members of Congress. By citing the source, teams can be specific about which plan they mean.

Policy recommendations offered by experts will more often than not fall within the realm of common knowledge. Those instances where common knowledge would be violated would be cases where a team cites a specific regional policy that has not garnered national attention. For example, the suggestion that there be mandatory parental punishment for juvenile offenders in Silverton, Oregon, would probably not be considered common knowledge.

However, California's three-strikes law certainly would fall into the domain of common knowledge. Of course, these cases are dependent on the knowledge of both teams and the judge. What may be common for one may not be for the others.

An additional area of expert testimony is the case of philosophical and political assumptions. Philosophical assumptions are theories about the way things are. While these assumptions are not necessarily evidence in and of themselves, they can help to prove a particular point in a case. When philosophical assumptions are used as evidence, they fall under the realm of expert testimony since the debaters rely on the expert philosophical knowledge of the philosopher in question. Suppose the resolution read *This House believes sexual preference should be protected by the Government*. The Opposition could claim that the purpose of the Government is to protect natural rights and that sexual preference is not a natural right as defined by John Locke. Therefore, sexual preference should not be protected. In this case, the argument itself is grounded in the expert testimony of Locke.

Whenever a claim is made, some form of evidence must be used to prove the claim. Without evidence, a claim is an assertion without proof. The whole purpose of argumentation is to set about proving claims. This cannot be done without evidence.

REASONING

Reasoning is the stated or unstated reasons why the claim should be accepted. Reasoning is not always stated point blank in a round. However, reasoning is essential to any argument. There are five methods of reasoning according to Gronbeck, German, Ehninger, and Monroe: inductive, deductive, sign, parallel case, and cause (269–71). We will briefly describe each of these types.

Inductive Reasoning

Inductive reasoning involves drawing a general conclusion by considering specific examples. Essentially, inductive reasoning looks at specific examples to draw conclusions about the class of objects. For example, if I say that politicians break the law, I can reach that conclusion by considering the examples of Richard Nixon, Bob Packwood, and Dan Rostenkowski. Inductive reasoning requires that you consider enough relevant examples to support the claim.

Deductive Reasoning

Deductive reasoning applies "a general conclusion to a specific example" (Gronbeck et al. 268). In effect, deductive reasoning follows the opposite path of inductive reasoning. If it is generally accepted that politicians are untrustworthy, I can logically conclude that most likely politician X will also be untrustworthy. Again, when using deductive reasoning, the speaker must be sure that the specific case fits the general category in order to fulfill the expectations of the category.

Sign Reasoning

Sign reasoning involves drawing conclusions from conditions that are observable or present during another state. For example, when the leaves of a tree begin to turn color, we reason that this is a sign that autumn must be near. This type of reasoning requires that the speaker be sure that one thing necessarily indicates another. One tree with brown leaves is probably not a sign that fall is coming since that tree may just be dead.

Parallel Case

Reasoning from a **parallel case** asserts that two cases are similar enough to draw conclusions about what must be true in both cases. This is also known as reasoning by analogy. We have already discussed analogies in the section on evidence. This type of reasoning follows that if two cases are substantially alike in relevant ways then what is true of one must be true of the other.

Causal Reasoning

Causal reasoning implies that one thing necessarily leads to another: Fire causes smoke. When using this type of reasoning, the speaker must be sure that the cause is integrally related to the effect. Causal reasoning relies on the logic that things happen in a predictable, reasonable progression.

Debates often consist almost entirely of teams arguing cause and effect. One team may argue that mandating the vote will cause an increased interest in one's representatives, while their opponents might counter that such mandates cause resentment and would have a negative impact on the country as a whole. As a parliamentary debater, you should always examine closely the connection among events. Experienced debaters often refer to it as "the link." You might hear someone claiming that "the Government hasn't shown us a link between pornography and crimes against women." The link refers to the connection between the two, or the causal law.

Be on the lookout for alternate causality. In other words, look for other possible causes for whatever effect has been mentioned. Most of the issues in debate deal with effects that have multiple causes. After hearing a claim of cause and effect by your opponents, ask yourself if there are other possible causes for the effect. Not only will this help you identify fallacious reasoning, but it will also stimulate counterarguments for your team.

The types of reasoning mentioned in this chapter are not necessarily stated explicitly in an argument. However, the connection between the claim and the evidence necessarily relies on some form of reasoning. One way to check the solidity of a case is to test the reasoning. If you are arguing, as asserted earlier, that politicians break the law, you might choose to argue using inductive reasoning. In this case, you would cite a few examples to support the claim. To check your reasoning, ask questions. Are you citing sufficient cases to prove the point? Can the Opposition cite different examples for all of your examples? By checking your reasoning process, you will tighten the wording of your claims (perhaps *Some politicians break the law* would be defended with more ease) and improve the quality of your evidence (more than three examples will probably be needed to prove the claim about politicians).

CONCLUSION

These are the basic elements of any argument. Not every argument is as simple as claim, evidence, and reasoning. However, no argument can go very far without these essentials. The next chapter will delve into the mechanics of how individual arguments work together to build a case. At this point, if you can be sure that for every claim you make you have evidence to prove the claim and reasoning to connect the two, you are far ahead of the game.

Chapter Three

Building Arguments

Key Concepts

Case—the totality of arguments that a team presents to prove
its side

Signpost—a phrase or term that indicates the relationship
between one concept and another

State, explain, support, conclude—an organizational pattern
to develop points in a speech requiring the speaker to state
the claim, explain what the claim means, offer evidence to
support the claim, and finally, show the implications of the
claim

Weighing mechanism—the standards by which the audience
evaluates the success of the Government and Opposition
cases [also known as *criteria*]

So, you've got a claim, you've got evidence, and you've got the reasoning that
connects the two. Now what? Come up with three good arguments.
Traditionally, constructive speeches have three contentions or claims. Each attempts to prove the resolution true or false from the perspective of the
Opposition. This chapter will begin with building an argument and then move
on to discuss how arguments work together to make a case.

INDIVIDUAL ARGUMENTS

Building a specific argument occurs in a four-step process: state, explain, support, and conclude. This is a simple process that has distinct advantages. Let us explore each of the steps.

State

The **state** step is simply the statement of the claim: *Politicians are not trustworthy.* The claim should be a simple declarative statement that establishes what you will attempt to prove. Claims that are long, involved, and flowery often confuse both the other team and the audience: "Those political malcontents, who clog the nations' Governmental machinery with extraneous spoutings, only thwart the common, decent citizen's ability to weed out the wheat from the chaff, and do not merit the trust of the United States public." Aside from the fact that there are four or five different claims in this statement, the audience has no clue as to what the speaker really means. Remember that when the Opposition must attack your case, it will need to identify specifically what it is attacking. Long, involved claims allow the Opposition to truncate the claim into a manageable statement. In so doing, the Opposition can word the simpler claim to its own advantage. Remember every salesperson's mantra: KISS—Keep It Simple, Stupid.

A related part of the claim is the signpost. A **signpost** is a phrase that shows the relationship of one point to other points in the argument or in the speech. An example of a signpost would be "Our first argument is. . . ." The signpost helps every person involved in the debate stay aware of where the speaker is. Since organization is a key to good debate, the use of signposts helps to keep a debate from becoming muddled.

Explain

The **explain** step involves elaborating on the intent of the claim. Often the reasoning is revealed in the explain step. For example, in the untrustworthy politician claim, you might explain the claim by saying, "If we look at politicians and their behavior over the past twenty-five years, we will find innumerable examples of instances where politicians have behaved in such a way as to earn the label 'untrustworthy.'" This explanation both sets up the inductive reasoning to follow and previews the type of evidence that will be used. Though the claim must be simple, the explanation allows the speaker to show the intricacies and implications of the argument.

Support

The **support** step provides the evidence used to prove the claim. Any of the forms of evidence may be used. In addition, more than one form of evidence may be used to support a point. And using a variety of methods of support will help to strengthen the claim of the argument. See Chapter Two for a more detailed discussion of argument.

Conclude

The **conclusion** of the argument not only wraps up the point but also shows the impact of that claim on the whole case. Consider the resolution *This House would install term limits.* If one of the Government's contentions is that politicians are untrustworthy, it might conclude that point by arguing, "As we've just shown, if politicians are untrustworthy, they should not be permitted to have unlimited access to congressional power without term limits." This conclusion allows the Opposition and the audience to see how the arguments work together.

The beauty of the state, explain, support, and conclude structure is that often the Opposition team will attack the evidence and leave the claim standing. The team that offers the claim can then provide more evidence to attempt to prove the claim. This can occur all the way through the Prime Minister's rebuttal. It is generally accepted that no new arguments may be brought up in rebuttal, but new examples are welcome. Consequently, you can still provide new evidence to help to prove a point all the way through the round of debate. The Prime Minister, then, still has the chance to win an argument with evidence that the Opposition cannot counter.

CASE

The **case** is the combination of arguments to prove or defeat a resolution. We will get into how Government teams create a case in the next chapter, but there is a basic structure that each speech will use. Because it is expected, it helps all of the members of the House follow the speech. The rest of this chapter provides basic guidelines for what to say, where, and when.

Introduction

The first thing a parliamentary debater does is recognize the participants in the debate. These introductions are an important part of parliamentary debate because they set the tone of the speech and the debate by beginning on a civil note. The most common introductions sound something like this: "I'd like to recognize the Speaker of the House (judge or instructor), my loyal Opposition, and my partner." Nicknames for partners or the opposing team are fine as long as the recognitions are not long or derisive. The recognitions begin each speech in a debate, even the rebuttals.

The actual introduction to a speech can begin with preliminary remarks or with the resolution. Either way is acceptable. Some debaters like to begin their speeches with a little story or an example to establish the mood and frame of their case. Speakers who choose this path should be sure that the story is short, simple, and easily connected to the case. Other debaters will begin directly with the resolution itself.

Definitions

Once the resolution is stated, the speaker will define the terms in the resolution. In cases of abstract topics, the definitions will be used in place of the abstract terms to make sense of what exactly is to be argued. More will be said about definitions in a later chapter.

Value and Criteria

The next step is to provide a value and a weighing mechanism or criteria.[1] The **weighing mechanism** provides criteria by which to judge if the teams have met their responsibility in regard to the resolution. This step is dependent on what type of resolution is being debated. The value allows the judge to see by what standard the round should be judged. For example, if the Government says it values equality, the judge knows to decide the outcome of the debate by determining which side provides more equality.

In some value debates, the values of each side are necessarily in conflict and the debate revolves around which is a more important value. In this case, the Government must provide criteria for determining which value is more important. Given the resolution *United States immigration policy should be guided by the*

---

[1] Not all coaches, judges, or teams believe that the value and criteria must be stated—they feel both of these are inherent in the case being presented. Nevertheless, stating them makes it clear to all participants, and unless you are very comfortable with the format, you should probably state both.

metaphor of the salad bowl rather than the melting pot, the sides are already divided by the values of diversity or commonality. To determine which is better, the Government must provide criteria, such as, "Which value better meets the needs of the majority of citizens?"

Arguments

To prove the resolution true, the Government then offers three (or occasionally two or four) independent arguments that support the resolution. Each of these arguments follows the state, explain, support, conclude guidelines. Once the arguments have been given, the Government shows how the case supports the value or meets the criteria. Later chapters will examine specifically how these cases can be developed.

Each speaker should follow the outline established by the Prime Minister. Skipping around or ignoring portions of a speech will only cause trouble for the speaker. We cannot stress enough the importance of organization. Organization is enhanced by signposting whenever possible. If you are the leader of the Opposition, you should label your points by saying, "The Government's first argument that states, 'Politicians are untrustworthy.'" In a sense, speakers should always assume that the audience just woke up, so the speaker must continually update listeners as to where they should be looking.

In cases where the Prime Minister is unorganized or does not label the arguments, it is the Opposition's right and duty to fill in the blanks for the audience. Whatever the Government fails to define or explain in its first speech, the Opposition can define or explain to its own advantage. We will discuss this later when we talk about the Opposition case. If the Government is unorganized, the Opposition will win points by clarifying the debate with organization.

Conclusion

Each speech should have a definite conclusion. As with any speech, the speaker should review the main points of the case and provide a strong ending statement that will leave a lasting, positive impression in the audience's mind about both the speaker and the case.

CONCLUSION

This, then, is the basic structure of how arguments work together. A beginning debater who follows this structure will be ahead of the game. Indeed, experienced speakers often forget these lessons and can lose a debate on technicalities because the debate was not clearly structured. Following this pattern will allow debaters to produce a case that proves or disproves a resolution. The content of what goes into the structure will be discussed in the two chapters on constructing Government and Opposition cases.

Chapter Four

Research

Since parliamentary debaters bring no physical evidence into a debate, you might assume that research is unnecessary. Quite the contrary, parliamentary debate requires a great deal of research. Debaters are expected to have a wide breadth of knowledge about a variety of topics in contrast to an in-depth knowledge of one subject area.

There are both advantages and disadvantages to this type of research need. Among the advantages is the student's ability to call on previously held knowledge. In addition, all of those baccalaureate core courses will come in handy.

Finally, students become well rounded in their knowledge of the world by researching current events, history, culture, and classical readings. The downside of this type of research need is that it can be an overwhelming task. How does a freshman acquire enough knowledge in a short amount of time to be prepared to debate almost any topic? There is no quick and easy answer. However, this chapter will attempt to create a manageable program for both the parliamentary debater and the student in an argumentation class.

In this chapter we outline five research areas students should cover: timeless questions, current events, history, philosophical and political assumptions, and resolution origin analysis.

TIMELESS QUESTIONS

Since the dawn of time, certain issues have existed that just can't be answered in any definitive fashion. "Why are we here?" is a good example. Although some people might suggest that they have the answers, chances are others will disagree. Questions that have plagued humans from the start rear their ugly heads in parliamentary debate as well; they are known as **timeless questions**. Anyone witnessing a season of parliamentary debate would recognize the repeated emergence of fundamental conflicts in many of the debates. Although the larger context surrounding these issues varies, often the same value clashes surface in rounds. Here are some examples of rudimentary conflicts that arise in parliamentary debate:

- The rights of the individual versus the power of the state
- Freedom of expression versus public concerns for decency
- Human rights versus national sovereignty

Experienced parliamentary debaters' argumentative repertoires will expand as they become more familiar with these issues through exposure in rounds. However, a participant taking the time to discover timeless issues *prior* to debates holds a distinct advantage.

If the United States Congress is debating the merits of a constitutional amendment to designate the burning of the American flag as an "unprotected expression subject to criminal sanctions," you should ask yourself what the fundamental issues underlying the debate seem to be. What is meant by "free expression"? What role does the symbolic nature of a flag represent? What is the purpose of a constitutional amendment? Is free expression more significant than patriotism?

This list suggests the kinds of elemental questions that must be examined by well-prepared debaters. It is your responsibility to prepare yourself for debates concerning such value conflicts.

Think of times when you have discussed controversies with friends and family. The more you revisit an area of controversy, the greater become both your understanding of the issue and your ability to anticipate the common lines of argument concerning the topic. Prior conscious deliberation of the topic area expands your argumentative repertoire and increases the likelihood you will argue effectively.

We recognize that timeless controversies are infinite and that complete anticipation and preparation remain unlikely. It would be disingenuous to give credence to the idea that a debater could anticipate every single controversy that might emerge. Nevertheless, attempting to discover and debate the most common value conflicts will provide you with a significant advantage over an unprepared competitor.

At this point, you may be thinking to yourself, "How do I discover these fundamental conflicts?" Fortunately for you, as a student pursuing a degree in an institution of higher education, you are in an ideal environment from which to observe and explore fundamental issues and conflicts. Unlike competitive sports, where athletes might view their coursework as time away from skill building for their preferred endeavor, parliamentary debate rewards those with the breadth of knowledge that is fostered by a liberal arts education. The knowledge and critical thinking skills gleaned from courses in history, philosophy, political science, literature, biology, chemistry, and every other subject you encounter during your educational journey will directly assist you in your parliamentary debating efforts. For example, you will encounter the controversy of nature versus nurture in basic biology and psychology courses. A wise parliamentary debater is one who views the classroom experience as an ideal environment in which to prepare and train for weekend debate tournaments. The timeless questions and spirited debates you encounter in your coursework provide you with a window into the historical background of important controversies and issues.

Once you have discovered some of these fundamental issues, it is time to do some reading. What have some of the most important political philosophers written about the role of free expression in a republic? What is the proper relationship between citizens and their government? Are human beings born with certain rights, or are they granted rights by their government? These and many other fundamental questions have been written about and debated extensively throughout history. Take advantage of the historical record by familiarizing yourself with the ideas of those who have debated these issues before you.

Remember also that viewing issues from nontraditional perspectives may be just as compelling as issues developed from a Eurocentric viewpoint. What do writers such as bell hooks, Camille Paglia, or Richard Rodriguez have to say? Often these perspectives will shed a different light on common assumptions and raise new issues that you might not encounter otherwise.

However, you should not take what has been written before you as the *only* arguments with merit. Use these theories and arguments as starting points for your own investigation and contemplation of the issues. What do *you* think about the justifications for war? Have the authors you have read missed some key issues? Are there other arguments that are more important? The time you spend thinking, arguing, and discussing these issues *before* debating will assist you when formulating your positions in an actual debate.

We suggest preparing solid stock cases concerning timeless philosophical dilemmas and holding them up for scrutiny in practice debates. This serves to further familiarize you and your partner with the myriad issues and examples inherent to potential topics, as well as to expose weaknesses in your understanding of and familiarity with the issues.

If you and your partner were to recognize that debates often center on the question of state sovereignty, in preparation you might construct a Government case defending this right. Practice sessions defending sovereignty would help you discover important issues, highlight the strengths and weaknesses of counterarguments, and give you practice in defending the value of the sovereign right of nations.

CURRENT EVENTS

Current events are economic, political, or social issues that are in the forefront of the public's attention at the present time. To prepare for potential current event topics, the parliamentary debater must have enough information to argue the history and issues of any given topic of current political, economic, or social interest. There are certain issues that students will encounter more often than other issues. These are topics about which debaters should have more information. These popular topics include welfare reform, affirmative action, gun control, environmental issues, big government versus decentralized government, media influence, and the American legal system. These issues have such far-reaching implications that they often appear in resolutions. In addition, topics that are stated abstractly often lend themselves to a discussion of these same issues.

A good parliamentary debater will read one weekly or monthly magazine (*The Economist, World Press Review*) and a daily paper (*New York Times, Washington Post, Christian Science Monitor*). Parliamentary debaters need to find a system that allows them to keep all of the information in their heads since carded evidence is not allowed in the round. Working with some system of summarizing and filing information is probably the easiest way to maintain a critical eye on the world.

Most people end up debating with a consistent partner. For maximum coverage, we suggest that you and your partner first engage in separate research. Organize it so that you examine different sources. Perhaps your partner enjoys reading the *New York Times*, watching CNN, and subscribes to *The Nation* magazine. Maybe you prefer the *Wall Street Journal*, C-SPAN, the *National Review*, and the Internet. (If you confine yourself to the Weather Channel you might wish to alter your habits a bit.) This contrast would be ideal. However, if you and your partner are not naturally drawn to distinct sources, create a plan fostering maximum coverage of the media spectrum. This way, when you get together with your partner, you will be prepared to compare and discuss your findings and report your perceptions on the major events and controversies you believe you might encounter in upcoming debates.

Follow up your discussion by assessing which controversies have clear value conflicts. Does a newly proposed Senate bill create tension between states' rights and those of the federal government? Does a recent story find a journalist's right to keep sources confidential in conflict with law enforcement's desire to apprehend suspected criminals? Since debate centers on clashes, actively seek out important news events and dissect them for important areas of conflict.

Although each partner must have some knowledge of all possible topics, one partner can learn certain topic areas in more detail in order to cover the necessary ground. Suppose Partner A is a political science major; that partner might already be well versed in international and domestic political issues. Partner B is a business major and keeps track of economic issues. Under these circumstances, Partner A need not spend a great deal of time trying to understand the intricacies of the budget deficit because Partner B has it covered. A wise team will spend some time talking about issues in which one member is well versed and the other is not. Such discussions will enable teams to act cohesively in rounds. The partner who is more expert in a subject should serve as Prime Minister or Leader of the Opposition. This role will change when the other partner's area of expertise is featured in a round.

It is easy to see how working with a partner will help with the workload of retrieving and absorbing the required information. In addition, teams can work together to produce **information logs**, which are brief summaries of important topics and issues. Information logs work something like this: The coaching staff or instructor produces a list of topics that every college student should know. Each member of the team is responsible for creating an information log that explains the topic. The log should be brief but thorough. Suppose someone was creating a log on affirmative action. The log might include a brief history that pinpoints the highlights of the evolution of affirmative action laws, a description of the current state of the law, and a discussion of the key arguments on both sides of the issue. This log might be two pages long. The information should not be as expansive as if you were writing a paper, but it should be sufficient to give your team the fundamentals from which to build a case. Teams that build these information logs can probably cover enough basic concepts to participate in parliamentary debate in just a few weeks. Each member of the team is responsible for reading and understanding each log created for the team.

Information logs alone are not sufficient research from which to build winning cases. However, they are a good starting point. To build winning cases, students need to have a real understanding of history, philosophy, and politics as well.

HISTORY

One of the primary forms of evidence used in parliamentary debate is the historical analogy. A **historical analogy** compares a historical event with a current event to project the probable outcome. For example, during the Gulf War, President Bush continually compared that war with Vietnam by saying, "This will not be another Vietnam." Bush's argument was that the Gulf conflict would not be a long, protracted war that would divide the U.S. public like Vietnam did. Those who argued against Bush's analogy had to have specific knowledge of what happened in Vietnam. Likewise in parliamentary debate, a fundamental knowledge of important historical events is necessary to either support or refute arguments.

Understanding certain key terms may be critical for proposing or refuting arguments. For example, can you define the Munich analogy, the McCarthy witch hunts, *Sputnik*, the fall of the Berlin Wall, the United Nations' Declaration on Human Rights? All had important influences on the course of our nation's recent history.

Information logs will include many of these events. However, there are certain documents of which all debaters should have a more extensive knowledge. The Universal Declaration of Human Rights is a prime example. The document itself is not that long or complicated; however, understanding the history and implications of the document does require deeper reading and probing.

PHILOSOPHICAL AND POLITICAL THEORIES

Since carded evidence is not permitted in parliamentary debate, most people assume that authority is not used in this format. This is not true. Authority is frequently used in the form of philosophical or political assumptions. **Theories of politics or philosophy**[1] often serve as the foundational justification for values or plans. Consequently, there are several theories that recur in rounds.

One of the most popular notions is the political and philosophical concept of natural law and natural rights. In a round debating an issue of human rights, John Locke's concept of natural law will almost assuredly make an appearance. Locke assumes that humans are basically friendly, peaceful folk who just want to get along. A Government team might use Locke as an expert to prove that human rights violations go against the grain of society. However, a good Opposition team will be able to argue Thomas Hobbes's theory of natural law which says that humans are conquerors and will seek to destroy each other for their own personal gain. In this way, the round acquires a complexity that arguing the mere surface of the issue will not foster.

---

[1] We might also include cultural, sociological, ontological, epistemological, axiological, and communication theories. In fact, there are a variety of theories and assumptions that could help in rounds. However, our purpose here is to provide the basics. Once you become experienced and comfortable with the basics, you will venture into these other areas.

There are certain theories that every good debater should know and understand. These include categorical imperatives, allegory of the cave, divine rights of man, and social contract theory. Again, with experience, you will come to an understanding of the most commonly cited theories.

Areas of history and philosophical and political assumptions are listed in Appendix B. Working on information logs on these topics will give the parliamentary debater the minimum knowledge necessary for a successful debating career.

RESOLUTION ORIGIN ANALYSIS

A final area of preparation for a parliamentary debater concerns analysis of the debating environment. Although you cannot read the mind of the authors of the propositions, you can certainly make educated guesses as to the subject areas you might find yourself debating. This guesswork goes beyond a thorough analysis of current events. Anticipating what the authors of the resolutions might do brings us into the third area of research and preparation: audience analysis or **resolution origin analysis**.

In the competitive parliamentary debating atmosphere, you would ask the following questions about the origin of the resolutions: Which college or university is hosting the tournament? Who will be in the tabulation room? Do you have an idea as to who will be writing the resolutions? Does your coach? If so, what do you know about these persons? Where do they live? Can you recall any controversies or events in that area of the country that have recently received media coverage?

An example of this would be the California ballot measure that outlawed bilingual education. This proposition generated enormous controversy in the state of California and garnered nationwide coverage. Parliamentary debate resolutions focusing on the issues inherent in this controversy were continually present at California debate tournaments. Try to put yourself in the shoes of the resolution writer. Scan regional newspapers and news sources that might clue you in to controversies germane to that area of the country.

What else do you know about the authors? What can you remember from ballots they have written? Does your coach know them personally? What are their areas of academic interest? Do they often research and write about mass media issues? Do they publish papers on feminist theory? Are they particularly interested in presidential rhetoric? Answers to these questions will help you to understand the resolution writers' interests and may give you a lead in the direction of potential resolutions.

Use the experience and knowledge your coach and senior team members possess. They are probably familiar with tournaments and might be able to tell you what types of resolutions have been used in the past. Even beyond the basic subject matter, some coaches prefer straightforward policy resolutions, while others may prefer the abstract types. Again, make the best use of the resources available to you.

In the argumentation classroom, your instructor may give you a list of potential areas. If not, you can start to guess at what kinds of resolutions that he or she might favor. Pay attention to the examples used in class. Does your instructor favor political examples? Social issues? What other classes does he or she teach? Answers to questions like these can reveal a great deal about areas in which your instructor has an interest. These are more likely areas for potential topics.

CONCLUSION

The five areas of research (timeless questions, current events, history, philosophical and political theories, and resolution origin analysis) should provide a solid grounding for the parliamentary debater. While no one person can know everything about every topic, if, between you and your partner, you research these areas, you will be more likely to be able to handle whatever topic comes your way. Research in parliamentary debate can be frustrating and overwhelming. However, even novice students will have a base of knowledge from which to argue. The beauty of this debate form is that it allows you to draw on resources you already have.

Chapter Five

Fallacies

Key Concepts

Ad hominem *fallacy*—attacking the person rather than the argument

Ad populum *fallacy*—claiming that something is true because popular belief dictates its truth

Ad verecundiam *fallacy*—an appeal to an authority who does not have expertise in the field at issue

Appeal to ignorance—claiming that something is correct because it has never been proven incorrect

Begging the question—asserting the premises as the conclusions to be proven

Equivocation—altering the meaning of a critical term during the course of a debate

Fallacy—reasoning that is faulty

False cause—erroneously attributing the cause of an outcome

False dilemma—reasoning that suggests there are only two possible options when in reality there are more than two options

Hasty generalization—generalizing on the basis of inadequate cases

Non sequitur—putting forth an irrelevant claim

Slippery slope—the assumption that one step will lead to additional steps that will lead to catastrophe

Straw man fallacy—defeating a position that the opposing team has not put forth as a strong or primary position

We discussed the nature of argument in Chapters Two and Three. We spoke of its basic components: evidence, reasoning, and claim, as well as the elements necessary for a well-constructed argument. We explained how a greater understanding of the entire process of argumentation will enable you to build and refute arguments in a parliamentary debate round. In addition to these elements of argumentation, it is crucial to understand faulty reasoning and poor argumentation in order to be able to argue against a case and defend a case effectively. In fact, parliamentary debaters who have a solid understanding of faulty argumentation will have an advantage over those who do not.

In the study of argumentation, errors or weaknesses in reasoning are referred to as **fallacies**. At first glance, many fallacious arguments appear reasonable, and most do have a strong psychological appeal. However, producing or accepting such arguments in a debate will damage your effectiveness and credibility as a speaker.

Therefore, in this chapter, we will discuss some of the fallacies that often occur in parliamentary debate. This is not meant to be a comprehensive list of reasoning errors. It merely serves as an attempt to identify common reasoning fallacies found in parliamentary debate, to explain them, and to provide suggestions for handling them in a debate.

HASTY GENERALIZATION

A **hasty generalization**, or "hasty G," as many debaters refer to it, consists of generalizing on the basis of inadequate cases or instances. Cases may be considered inadequate because these cases are either too few or perhaps unrepresentative of the larger class of objects. An example on the subject of health care illustrates a hasty generalization: "I read of a case in Canada where a woman had to wait two months before she was able to have an operation she desperately needed. Socialized medicine simply doesn't work." Making a general claim about the effectiveness of socialized medicine based solely on the single example of this woman would be a hasty generalization. We simply cannot logically infer the adequacy of Canada's health care system from one woman's experience.

If your opponents employ this type of faulty reasoning, it is not enough to identify it as a hasty generalization in your next speech. You should explain to the audience exactly how and why your opponent's claim is invalid. "Mr. Speaker, the Prime Minister attempts to indict the entire health care system in the country of Canada by pointing to one single example, which may or may not be accurate. We on this side of the aisle recognize that individual cases may be unrepresentative of the whole and ask that you recall the numerous examples we have provided illustrating the strengths of such a system. The Government's argument fails to legitimize the claim and therefore does not support its case."

FALSE CAUSE

Another typical reasoning fallacy in parliamentary debate is often referred to as **false cause**. There are two types of false cause fallacies: single cause and *post hoc ergo propter hoc*, "after this, therefore because of this." Single-cause fallacies occur when the speaker erroneously assumes that one condition or action is the result of another condition or action. An example of the reasoning fallacy of single cause is "Violent video games are the cause for the rise in school violence." Certainly, other causes may contribute to the rise in school violence.

Post hoc ergo propter hoc fallacies occur when sequence is confused with causation. Because one event follows another, it is assumed that the first event caused the second event. An example of this fallacy was uttered by my neighbor: "Of course it's beginning to rain—I just finished washing my car." This poor fellow has just committed the *post hoc* fallacy. He's identified the cause of the weather (the reason it is raining) as the action of washing his car. Simply because the rain fell after he finished washing his car, the act of washing the car did not cause the rain to fall. It is true that sometimes an effect will immediately follow its cause (e.g. the skier fell and broke her leg) but this is not always the case. To avoid this fallacy, a debater needs to invoke a causal law that connects events of one type with those of another. We have no law connecting car washing and rain.

APPEAL TO IGNORANCE

Still another fallacy common to parliamentary debate rounds is that of the **appeal to ignorance**. This reasoning fallacy consists of arguing that a claim is right because it has never been demonstrated to be wrong. When your opponent stands at the podium and claims, "Madame Speaker, no major studies have shown us why a six-year presidential term is a bad idea. This indicates to us that it is a favorable plan, and we strongly urge you to support it." This debater has just committed an appeal to ignorance. Establishing claims by argument necessitates presenting reasons for it. A supposed absence of reasons against something is very different from having reasons for it.

Simply pointing out to the audience the logical flaw involved in the appeal to ignorance will help to clarify why indeed no good case has been made by your opponents. Following this with counterarguments will further strengthen your position against your opponent.

AD POPULUM FALLACY

Fallacious reasoning in parliamentary debate often takes the form of appeals to popular beliefs or attitudes. As the name implies, an *ad populum* **fallacy** occurs when someone claims that something is correct simply for the reason that it is generally believed to be true. Though this may sound like a simple fallacy to detect, you should be forewarned that this fallacy takes many forms and can easily catch a debater unaware. An example on welfare exhibits this fallacy quite clearly. "We all know that one of the primary reasons the United States federal government has such an enormous budget deficit every fiscal year is that too much is spent on foreign aid." This is a commonly held belief but simply not an accurate one. The United States devotes less than one percent of expenditures to foreign aid. A debater using this appeal to a popularly held belief may have reminded you that many Americans hold this belief, but he has not proven his claim that foreign expenditures are a primary reason for the budget deficit every year.

Pointing out specific examples where the perception of the general population was at odds with reality is also an effective counter to such an argument. History is replete with examples wherein the general belief, or conventional wisdom, is simply wrong. An early example is the belief in a geocentric (earth-centered) as opposed to the accurate heliocentric (sun-centered) universe. The fact that many people believe something to be so is not enough to logically accept it as true.

FALSE DILEMMA

Another fallacy consistently evident in parliamentary debate is that of the **false dilemma**. This fallacy implies that there is only an either/or choice in a given situation. In reality there may be other options. Consider "You must side with either the Democrats or the Republicans." Although sometimes it would seem that these are your only choices in the United States, of course the dilemma presented is a false one because several other parties exist. A person might vote for a registered independent or even choose not to support any side at all. The point is that the array of choices presented in the argument are falsely limited. Alarm bells should ring when your opponents claim that only two competing possibilities exist.

SLIPPERY SLOPE

The **slippery slope** contains the idea that one misstep will cause a slide down the entire mountain. For instance, one of the prominent arguments against any type of gun control follows this kind of reasoning: Should the United States Congress put a limitation on any types of firearms, it would inevitably lead to a complete ban on all firearms. The attractiveness of such an argument is obvious. Incremental changes can evolve into major changes. The fallacy lies in the belief that the evolution is inevitable. Be on the alert for this fallacy, as it is very common in parliamentary debate rounds.

BEGGING THE QUESTION

Begging the question occurs when debaters take as the premises for their arguments the very conclusions they wish to illustrate. An example of begging the question is "Toni Morrison is a controversial writer because people can't agree about her writing." This is clearly an instance of circular reasoning. Debaters should be especially alert for this fallacy during the explanation of a case. Many a Government team has attempted to win a debate by pronouncing a case statement that exemplifies this fallacy.

AD VERECUNDIAM FALLACY

The appeal to inappropriate authority or ***ad verecundiam* fallacy** seeks to illustrate the legitimacy of a position by pointing to the support of an exalted individual or group. The fallacy exists when the individual or group identified lacks expertise in the area cited. In this age of celebrity worship, examples of *ad verecundiam* are common. Unfortunately, many media-saturated debaters point to inappropriate authorities to support their claims. Beware of debaters using fictional movies and television programs as support. For instance, the film *Mr. Holland's Opus* is not a legitimate authoritative source to support claims for educational reform.

STRAW MAN

The **straw man fallacy** is committed when a speaker holds up a weaker version of an argument used by an opponent, refutes it, and claims to have defeated the opponent's larger position. In some cases, a straw man fallacy is committed by asserting a position that the opposing team has not made and then defeating that position. A Prime Minister asserts that the environmental impact should be the first concern of any policy. The Leader of Opposition then argues that the Government has claimed that environmental impact is the *only* concern in policymaking.

EQUIVOCATION

The fallacy often referred to as **equivocation** may be one of the most common in parliamentary debate. Equivocation occurs when the meaning of a critical term changes during the course of the argument. Debaters often refer to a "case shift" when a team attempts to change the meaning of a key term in the debate during the course of the round. A team defining the term *free expression* as "completely unrestricted speech" early on in the debate only to change it to "mostly unrestricted speech" during the course of the debate has committed the fallacy of equivocation. The frequency of such incidents in parliamentary debate highlights the significance of the careful definition of terms during the constructive speeches of the debate.

NON SEQUITUR

When former baseball player Pete Rose was denied induction into the Baseball Hall of Fame for his conviction of illegal gambling, many Rose supporters argued that his conviction was irrelevant to the decision of whether or not he should be a Hall of Famer. These fans were in a sense claiming that supporters of the ban were guilty of the fallacy known as ***non sequitur***. *Non sequitur* translates to "does not follow" and identifies claims that do not reasonably follow from the data or arguments offered as support. Rose's supporters believed that his being a convicted felon was irrelevant to his induction because that honor should be based on his contributions on the playing field.

AD HOMINEM

The final fallacy we will discuss might be the least pleasant and we hope the least frequently employed in parliamentary debate. We are talking about the ***ad hominem* fallacy**. *Ad hominem* translates to "against the person" and occurs when a speaker attacks the person rather than the argument. In parliamentary debate, *ad hominem* attacks are strictly forbidden, and debaters often lose credibility when such attacks are employed. Debaters on the receiving end of such attacks may rise to a point of personal privilege if the perception is that they have been the recipient of a personal attack. The Speaker of the House will make a ruling on the legitimacy of the claim.

CONCLUSION

In this chapter, we have identified some of the reasoning fallacies that occur in parliamentary debate and given suggestions for handling or countering such claims. We strongly advocate familiarizing yourself with the distinctions between legitimate and fallacious arguments.

Part II

Elements of Cases

Chapter Six

Government Responsibilities

Key Concepts

Burden of debatability—a Government responsibility to interpret the resolution so that both Government and Opposition have a fair opportunity to debate

Burden of proof—a Government responsibility to prove the resolution true

Burden of topicality—a Government responsibility to develop a case that is germane to the given resolution

Common knowledge—information that is widely available and known by the average college student

Constructive speech—a speech used to build a case

Ground—the specific case area that a team must defend

Truism—a resolution that is interpreted to prove itself

In parliamentary debate, it is the burden of the Government team to support the resolution. Following the historical model of the houses of Parliament, the Government team attempts to persuade the members of Parliament to vote for the motion being considered. The Government team consists of the Prime Minister and the Member of Government. The Prime Minister is responsible for the first seven-minute **constructive speech** and the final five-minute rebuttal. The Member of Government is responsible for an eight-minute constructive that follows the Leader of the Opposition's constructive speech; it is the third constructive speech in the debate. To understand the elements of the Government's case, we must consider first an overview of the Government team's responsibilities.

OVERVIEW OF GOVERNMENT RESPONSIBILITIES

The National Parliamentary Debate Association (NPDA) guidelines state, "It is the responsibility of the Government to define and defend the resolution in a manner which makes it debatable." Therefore, the Government in a parliamentary debate meets its burden by accomplishing three goals:

- The Government must prove the resolution true.
- The Government must define the terms of the resolution.
- The Government must provide a debatable case.

There are various methods of doing each of these charges, but first we must understand what each of these burdens means.

Foremost in any debate, the adjudicator will ask whether the Government team has proven the resolution to be true.[1] For any given resolution, this means that the House would adopt the resolution. This is known as the **burden of proof.** In any situation, the party asserting the claim has the burden to prove that it is true. For example, given the resolution *This House would reform the welfare system*, the judge must be able to say at the end of the debate that the Government has proven that the welfare system should be reformed.

The second burden is to define terms. At the very beginning of the Prime Minister's constructive, she should define the terms in the resolution (see Chapter Eight). This means that the Government must provide parameters for what the resolution means as a whole. This is done by defining the terms. Should the Government team define *all* terms in the resolution? In his explanation of parliamentary debate, Robert Trapp writes, "One need not define every term in the motion in order to explain its meaning; one need only define the

---

[1] Depending on the nature and content of the resolution, the adjudicator may ask different types of questions, such as, "Has the Government defended the resolution, supported the resolution, and proven the policy should be adopted?" For our purposes here, "proving the resolution true" is a catchall phrase.

most important and abstract terms" (NPDA). While this is certainly true in the vast majority of cases, a truly careful Government team might define every term to protect itself from wily Opposition teams seeking an advantage. Some Opposition teams will attempt to define "the House" as a body unsympathetic to the arguments put forth by the Government team. Some audiences will find this practice obnoxious; others will deem it clever and reward it with acceptance.

The degree of latitude afforded the Government in terms of its definitions and case building is audience-dependent. If the Prime Minister's arguments justify the Government's interpretation of the resolution and the audience believes the case is debatable, the Government has met their **burden of topicality**. Topicality is the burden to debate within the constraints of the given topic and to present a case that links to the resolution. Topicality in policy debate, according to Michael Pfau, David A. Thomas, and Walter Ulrich, "poses a jurisdictional question" (153). Essentially, topicality serves several functions in the debate. First, topicality provides the parameters of the debate. The Government team is required to establish a specific case within the bounds of the resolution. This requirement implies that the Government should maintain the spirit of the resolution. The second requirement of topicality is that the Government in its case development establishes the demarcation of sides in the debate. This ensures that the proposition remains debatable. These requirements lead to the *a priori* nature of the topicality standard. The Government must maintain the burden of topicality in order to make the debate fair. This requirement must be met before any other Government burden or case can even be considered.

The nature of parliamentary debate alters the burden of topicality for several reasons. First, resolutions are often an odd combination of quotations, clichés, straight resolutions, and other material. Consequently, a Government team often has great latitude in interpreting the resolution. This has a substantial impact on the burden of topicality for the Government team. Of course, some judges are more lenient than others in their assessment of the legitimacy of the Government's resolutional analysis and case interpretation. Regardless of the specific interpretation of the resolution employed by the Government, the Prime Minister should provide a logical justification for the perceived legitimacy of that interpretation. It does not suffice for the Prime Minister to declare that as Government, it is the Prime Minister's prerogative to define the terms. The link to the resolution necessitates a cogent argument by the Prime Minister. Of course, when the diversity of resolutions creates so many possible interpretations by the Government, a central question becomes, "How do I choose my case?" This question leads us to the third burden of the Government team, providing a debatable case.

Like most entities struggling for survival, successful Government teams will limit their burdens. Why choose to defend a 10-foot-wide goal when one that is 5 feet wide will do? Government teams should ask themselves during the fifteen-minute preparation period, "What does the resolution require that we prove?" Students should seek to locate the minimal burden possible that still allots the Opposition debatable ground, a key element of the Government case.

Parliamentary debate requires that the Government team interpret the resolution in such a way as to provide for specific debate. Take the resolution *This House believes blue is better than red*. The wording of the resolution can only lead to an amorphous argument without any clear method of deciding the outcome. Consequently, the Government's burden is to link the resolution to a case that will lead to sound debate. In the blue/red resolution, the Government could easily link the case to democracy versus communism or any other governmental system. The key here is to understand the relationship of terms in the resolution to each other, thereby effectively linking the resolution to a case that maintains its spirit in advancing a debatable case.

This **burden of debatability** is important for several reasons. First, with the introduction of abstract resolutions, it is much more likely that the Government will encounter propositions that do not clearly spell out the issue to be debated. Consequently, it is the Government's burden to provide a debatable resolution, or at least to interpret the resolution to make it debatable.

The Government must provide fair ground for both teams. We can begin with the obvious charge to provide Opposition ground. It is tempting as a Government strategy to interpret the resolution to minimize the opposition's argumentative ground. Indeed, smart Government teams will attempt to pigeonhole the Opposition into arguing a weak position. This is a fine strategy. Most often a weak team will fall for the ploy and will easily be defeated by a strong Government team that sets the trap. The Government gets itself into trouble when it fails to provide *any* Opposition ground.

Failing to provide Opposition ground can occur for three reasons. First, the Government can interpret the resolution truistically. A **truism** occurs when the claim is obviously true or noncontroversial. For example, imagine the resolution *This House believes that child abuse is bad*. The Opposition is put in the untenable position of having to argue that child abuse is good. While some crafty teams might be able to construct a case to oppose the Government's link, this interpretation of the resolution is abusive in its burden on the Opposition.

The second reason that the Opposition can find itself without **ground** occurs when the Government places the Opposition in a morally repugnant position, as illustrated in the child abuse example.

Finally, the Opposition may find itself in a bind when faced with a case requiring specific knowledge. This often occurs when the Government assumes that what is general or **common knowledge** in Nebraska is also common knowledge in California. When the Government chooses to limit the debate to the merits of a specific case, that case must be widely publicized so that all parties have an equal opportunity to know the facts of the case. For example, given the resolution *This House believes the juvenile criminal justice system should be revamped*, the Government team from Willamette University in Salem, Oregon, might choose to debate the merits of the recent Silverton, Oregon, law that fines parents for juvenile crimes. Although the Government would be required to spell out the generalities of the Silverton law, the Opposition, if from say, Houston, would be at a decided disadvantage in arguing the merits of the law.

The Opposition could easily defend its rights by pointing out the abuses inherent in a given case. The Government in turn is left to defend its interpretation and will often lose the debate based on these abuses. Clearly, it is to the advantage of the Government to interpret the resolution so as to provide fair Opposition ground.

Equally important for the Government, but perhaps not as obvious, is the Government's burden to provide fair ground from which the Government itself can argue. Because of the nature of parliamentary debate, the Government has at most fifteen minutes to develop a case. Often the Government finds itself in the unenviable position of having to produce a plan and account for all the possible holes in a case in those same fifteen minutes. The Government is then charged with interpreting the resolution so as to limit the debate to enable the Government to defend the resolution in as fair a manner as possible.

The Government's burden then is to limit the resolution so that the Government is not charged with having to defend a whole system but rather part of the system. This is an especially important responsibility in the case where the resolution is poorly worded. Examine the resolution *This House believes that property rights are the root of society's evils*. The Government team might fail to limit the topic, and the Opposition could easily force the Government to defend the idea that every single evil in society can be traced to property rights.

Granted, the wording of the resolution would lead the Government to believe that defending that ground is its burden. However, to make for a good and reasonable debate, the Government would be well within its rights to interpret the resolution to mean that some *major* ills of society could be traced to property rights. The Government could then go on to proclaim those ills: racism, gang warfare, and homelessness. Certainly, this is a reasonable interpretation of the resolution and a much fairer ground from which to argue.

The Government must be assertive in its use of interpretation so as to limit the debate to make it fair for both sides. The Government must be cautioned that in limiting the interpretation of the topic, it does not define the Opposition out of the debate. By providing ground for both the Opposition and the Government to argue, the Government has provided a debatable case, thereby meeting its burden.

CONCLUSION

Though it would be easy to dismiss these as easy goals to achieve, the members of the Government team would be wise to ask themselves before speaking whether their case proves the resolution true, defines the terms of the resolution, and provides debatable ground for both cases. These are three elements that can be attacked easily by the Opposition. We will delve further into each of these issues in later chapters in Part II. However, understanding what the Government is attempting to achieve in its case provides a frame from which to view succeeding chapters on case construction.

Chapter Seven

Opposition Burdens

Key Concepts

Clash—the burden of the Opposition to argue against what the Government has proposed

"Even/if" analysis—an approach to a case that dictates that a team can object to the overall case based on procedural rules but cannot still debate the particulars

Link—the connection between the case and the resolution

Off case—independent Opposition assertions why the resolution should not be adopted

Presumption—the concept that assumes that without significant reason to change, no action should be taken

Status quo—the current state of affairs

The primary task of the Opposition team is to counter the motion and clash directly with the Government case. Although these burdens may seem straightforward, they hide some complex relationships and assumptions. In this chapter, we will discuss these burdens and some of the concepts that aid the Opposition in meeting its burdens.

COUNTERING THE RESOLUTION

The Opposition can approach countering the resolution in one of two ways. First, the Opposition can merely refute the Government's assertions. In this instance, if the Government case is defeated, there are no compelling reasons to believe the resolution is true, and the Opposition wins the debate. The reason this occurs is the notion of *presumption*, the assumption that without compelling reasons to change an established course of action or alter a belief, the **status quo** is adequate. When this happens, the debate falls to the Opposition. Presumption is tricky in parliamentary debate, where the type of resolution varies according to the wording of the resolution. A lengthy discussion of presumption is necessary here so that the Opposition team can understand its options in defeating a Government case.

Presumption is the term that specifies who occupies the figurative ground at the beginning of the debate. The classic example of presumption occurs in the American legal system, which identifies defendants as innocent until proven guilty. In the status quo, the defendant is innocent, and it is therefore incumbent on the prosecution to prove otherwise.

Parliamentary debaters must understand where presumption lies since presumption is not always granted outright to the Opposition team. Presumption is dependent on the type of resolution being debated. In policy debate, Pfau, Thomas, and Ulrich assert that presumption is "based on the risk of uncertainty. . . . If an affirmative change entails less risk than a negative alternative . . . then that affirmative should enjoy presumption" (239). Indeed, in value and factual rounds, presumption may not exist. Wood and Midgley argue that even if presumption is claimed by the affirmative [Government], it is not exempt from the burden of proof (91). Presumption is another issue that the world of parliamentary debate has yet to tackle in full force. However, the concept of presumption is crucial to creating and defending both Opposition and Government cases.

The second approach to defeating the resolution is not only to refute the Government's claims (which must be done regardless of the Opposition approach) but also to produce independent reasons why the resolution should not be upheld, known as the **off case**. This method has distinct advantages when adopted in conjunction with the former approach. First, just refuting the Government's case does not ensure that you will win on all arguments. In fact, rarely does one team clearly win every single argument. Without independent reasons why the resolution should not be adopted, if the Government wins even one minor argument, on balance, the judge may find that one argument more compelling than no arguments against the resolution. Second, in a close debate, independent reasons give the judge one more way to justify declaring an Opposition win. Attacking the Government case and providing an off case is a two-pronged attack that is likely to leave doubt in the judge's mind about the Government case.

CLASH

The second burden of the Opposition is to clash with the Government case. **Clash** is the idea that the Opposition must refute the Government case directly. This is a difficulty in parliamentary debate. **Link**—the connection between the resolution as stated and the case offered by the Government—is a particularly volatile issue when it comes to this form of debate. Abstract topics often lead the Government to places where the Opposition cannot anticipate the content of the Government's case. For example, the resolution *This House would rock the boat* leaves no clue as to the substance of the Government's case. Consequently, the Opposition can argue that the Government's case is not a reasonable link to the resolution, and the Opposition can then offer a different interpretation of the resolution. This is akin to ships passing in a fog. Too often debates resort to arguments over whose definitions are better while the cases themselves are left behind. Definitional debates, which most audiences and debaters hate, are usually the fault of the Opposition for not offering clash. This is not to say that the Opposition cannot raise objections to definitions offered by the Government. However, the Opposition must still proceed with an "even/if" analysis.[1]

The **"even/if" analysis** says, "We object to the case the Government has given us for the following reasons. . . . However, even if we accept the Government's case, which we do not, we will still find that there are problems with the case itself." What this does is allow the Opposition to raise doubt in the judge's mind about the fairness of the Government's case. In addition, the Opposition can then prove that the case itself is not sound. This provides clash in the round and gives the judge ample reason to vote for the Opposition. Without clash, the judge is left to judge only on whether the Government case is reasonable. If the judge finds that the Government case is reasonable and the Opposition has argued only that it is not, the Opposition loses.

---

[1] The only instance in which it is reasonable for an Opposition team to avoid clashing directly with the Government's case as presented occurs when the Government case is truistic or tautological. In either case, the Leader of Opposition should state explicitly that the Government's interpretation of the resolution is truistic, justify this interpretation, and offer an alternative case for the debate.

BUILDING A CASE

The Opposition must meet the burdens of disproving the resolution (or defeating the Government case) and providing clash. At the same time, the Opposition must remember that it, too, must provide a case within which these burdens are met. Remember that when you are opposing a resolution, it is vital to have an overarching philosophical position from which to argue. This is true regardless of the type of resolution being debated. Having a comprehensive philosophy will make it much easier to follow another basic principal: having an offensive position in addition to a defensive one.

Refutation from a constructive basis should be the strategic objective of the Opposition team—to use the old sports cliché, the best defense is a good offense. When constructing the Opposition case, debaters must remember to do just that, construct a case! Refutation is most powerful when it comes from the perspective of a viable constructive position.

On the resolution *This House supports term limits for Supreme Court justices*, debaters on the Opposition should seek to establish a consistent position that opposes the basic tenets of the resolution that has been presented. Creating a case that supports lifetime tenure for Supreme Court justices would create a situation wherein the Opposition is not only attacking the Government case but arguing *for* something as well. This strategic approach is potentially far more persuasive than simply launching a direct attack on the Government case.

CONCLUSION

Providing clash and countering the resolution are two elements of the Opposition case that should not be forgotten. Indeed, they are the *raison d'être* for the Opposition team. In fact, without these elements, we would not have a debate.

Chapter Eight

Defining the Resolution

Key Concepts

Assignment of burdens—the determination of who must argue what

Clarity—the clear determination of what is to be debated

Debatability—how the resolution will be debated in terms of fact, value, or policy

---

Imagine a debate on the resolution *Red is better than blue*. Suppose the Government team decided to debate the case as stated and proceeded to create a list of things that were red. It could list lips, roses, and sunsets. The Opposition would have to argue that blue roses, blue lips, and blue sunsets were better. Or it could argue, "Yes, those red things are lovely, but what about blue forget-me-nots, blue eyes, or blue skies?" Not only does the debate become a series of lists, but it is also frivolous. Indeed, had the Government defined *red* as socialism and *blue* as democracy, the debate would be one of competing values and would have produced a debate rich in philosophy, history, and substantive argumentation. Even though this example is a bit extreme, it illustrates the importance of defining the terms of the resolution.

One of the first steps that both the Government and Opposition teams must take in attempting to debate a particular resolution is to define the terms in the resolution, thus making it debatable. It is the Government's right and responsibility to define because it has the burden of proof and thus must establish what it must prove. If the Government unfairly delineates what it must prove or does not establish this at all, the Opposition then has the right to redefine or clarify the parameters for the debate. In this chapter, we will outline why it is important to define the terms of the debate and will discuss ways of defining.

WHY WE DEFINE

In any given resolution, there is bound to be at least one term that is ambiguous in its implications and meanings. Consequently, we must define terms in the resolution for three reasons: clarity (what), debatability (how), and assignment of burdens (who).

By **clarity** we mean that definitions clearly establish what is being debated. Both abstract and straight resolutions can often be interpreted in a variety of ways. Both Government and Opposition teams should decide what they think the resolution is asking the Government to prove. The Government establishes exactly what it is seeking to prove by defining the terms. In our example, by defining the terms *red* and *blue* as socialism and democracy, respectively, the Government has more clearly determined the subject of the debate.

When the Government team defines the terms of the resolution, they have also established the **debatability** of the resolution. By clearly establishing what the debate is to be about, the Government sets the type of debate that will ensue: fact, value, or policy. Clearly, the socialism-versus-democracy debate is a value debate because the Government will not only define *red* and *blue* but also establish a threshold for "better than." In this case, the Government might define "better than" as meaning that socialism provides for a better quality of life for its people. Hence, quality of life becomes the value to which socialism and democracy will be held. In this sense, the definitions have determined the argumentative ground each side should debate. This leads directly into the third reason we define: **assignment of burdens**.

Defining the terms of the resolution not only establishes what is to be debated and how but also who must prove what. The definitions as assigned to the resolution should establish the burdens for each team. Beyond the burdens as explored in Chapter Seven, in each debate the Government and Opposition will have additional ground to defend. Definitions establish this ground. In our sample resolution as defined, the Government must defend the idea that socialism provides a better quality of life for its people than democracy does. For its part, the Opposition must clearly assert that democracy provides at least equal quality of life for its people. Note that because the resolution asks the Government to prove *better than*, the Opposition can win by proving that the two systems are equal, for if they are equal, one cannot be better than the other.

To reiterate the importance of defining, let us apply our analysis to a straight resolution, *This House believes public schools should require school uniforms.* This looks obvious at first and seemingly doesn't need definition. But a closer examination reveals that without definitions, the debate could be quite messy. For example, by "public schools" do we mean K–12 or are we referring to public college? Do we mean that everyone must wear the exact same manufacturer's clothing or merely the same style? Can students wear their own socks, or are these regulated as well? If the Government does not define these terms in the beginning of its case, the debate can go in an unintended direction. The Opposition can proceed to spend the Leader of Opposition's speech explaining why college students do not need to wear uniforms when all of the Government's arguments focused on K–12. In addition, without defining the terms, the Opposition could choose to make the *uniform* so amorphous as to make it ineffectual, thus denying the round debatablility. Finally, by not limiting the terms of the debate, the Government has to defend more ground than the resolution or case required.

HOW TO DEFINE

When a team first considers a resolution, it should ask what the resolution requires it to prove. From there, the team can begin to define the terms to limit the ground of the debate. With working definitions in mind, the team members can then develop their case. However, before they enter the debating chambers, they should check their working definitions against the case to ensure that the definitions encompass what is being debated. For example, examine the resolution *This House would help the middle class.* If during prep time, you defined *middle class* as households with an annual income between $30,000 and $50,000 yet much of your argumentation focused on programs and tax breaks for families below the poverty line, you will leave yourself vulnerable and sounding quite silly. Refinement of definitions makes the case stronger in the long run. In much the same way that the reason that we debate is answered by looking at the what, the how, and the who, how we define terms can also be established by considering these same factors.

The next step a team should take in defining a resolution is to establish what is to be debated. To establish what should be the subject of the debate, teams should consider the relationship of terms (nouns) in the resolution. Though we will consider this idea at greater length in later chapters, for the purpose of this chapter the relationship between terms provides an immediate charge to the debater. For example, in the red-versus-blue resolution, it is clear that A and B are of the same category. Hence, the resolution requires that the argument center around a comparison of two like things. It would be unwise for the Government to define *red* as socialism and *blue* as the Republican party, a comparison of apples and oranges. A proper comparison would be socialism versus capitalism.

Likewise, the verb phrase will help the teams determine how they should debate the resolution. By verb phrase we mean the verb and any words that go with it. For example, "is better than" would be a verb phrase. In defining the verb phrase the Government team should clarify the type of debate (policy or value) and the threshold for determining the winner of the debate. If the resolution is worded as a comparison ("better than," "would rather," "either/or") the comparison will most likely lead to a value debate. The Government must establish then how the comparison is to be judged. If the resolution is worded as an action ("should make," "would exterminate," etc.) the Government must define that action specifically. If the resolution were *This House would reform the welfare system,* the Government could define "would reform" by saying, "By reform we mean to create a major change by moving to a system of workfare."

Regardless of how the terms in the resolution are defined, the Government should make sure to leave ground for both sides in the debate. Suppose that in the red and blue resolution where red is socialism, the Government defined the phrase "better than" as meaning that each person must be provided for equally. This in essence creates a tautology, since the threshold is the same definition as one of the terms. If socialism's goal is to provide for all people equally and the threshold for determining which is better is to see who provides equally, the Opposition cannot win the debate by defending democracy, which has no such guarantees.

In the same vein, when arguing policy resolutions, the Government team must provide a case that leaves room for the Opposition to argue. Look at the resolution *This House believes children should be allowed to be children.* A Government team could run a variety of cases that provide for children to be sheltered from the harsh realities of our world. A team could run a case that prohibits them from working before the age of eighteen, or a team could argue that children should wear uniforms to school so that distracting fashion competition is limited. In contrast, a Government team could not run a case that says, "We should stop child abuse by arresting anyone who is caught abusing a child." First, the Government is left defending the status quo, but even more problematic is that the Opposition is left defending child abusers, an untenable position.

As we said at the beginning of this section, the last thing a team should do before entering the debating chambers is to compare the definitions to the case to ensure that the case does not contradict the definitions. Often a simple readjusting of the wording will make the definitions consistent with the case. An example will illustrate its importance. Given the resolution *This House believes royalty is irrelevant,* a team might define royalty as persons who were born into a monarchy. However, should this team continually cite Princess Diana, who was royalty only by marriage, the case could easily be defeated by illustrating that the Government team was failing to provide examples that prove its point. A simple adjustment of the definitions to include people who married into the monarchy could save the case for this team.

The Opposition team should ask these same questions when considering the Government case. Has the Government determined clearly what is to be debated? Has the Government team established how the round will be decided? Has the Government team established who must prove what? If any of these questions remain unanswered or are not answered reasonably, the Opposition must provide new definitions. Consider the children resolution. If the Government provides the case that child abusers should be thrown in jail, the Opposition must explain why the definition is abusive and then provide a more reasonable definition. To make this particular resolution and interpretation debatable, the Opposition would have to either completely redefine the ground of the debate (perhaps changing it to school uniforms) or create an extreme position (which is often just as abusive). For instance, the Opposition could claim that the Government's case must be interpreted to mean that offenders will be sentenced to life in prison without parole. Although this is still not a good interpretation, at least there is some room for debate.

CONCLUSION

A quality debate requires well-thought-out definitions. This chapter has considered why definitions are important and some ways to go about creating useful ones. In many a debate round, the result has centered on how the terms of the resolution were defined. Savvy debaters will pay careful attention to how they and their opponents define terms.

Chapter Nine

Propositions of Fact and Value

While the general objective of defeating your opponents through superior argumentation and persuasion remains constant, the form your case takes should
be the product of analysis of the debate resolution you encounter. Many argumentation and debate theorists place resolutions into three separate categories:
fact, value, and policy (Freeley; Hill and Leeman; Ericson et al.; Winkler et al.).
However, we concur with Ziegelmueller and Kay who claim that distinguishing between fact and value is ". . . unnecessary because the methods of analyzing the issues are the same for both" (Ziegelmueller and Kay 20). Moreover, the
strategic approaches for both supporting and defeating propositions of fact and
value remain equivalent. With this in mind, in this chapter we discuss ap-

proaches for both supporting and defeating resolutions of fact and value in parliamentary debate.

FACT AND VALUE REQUIREMENTS

We look to Ziegelmueller and Kay who define resolutions of fact or value as "descriptive, predictive, or evaluative statements that assert the existence or worth of something" (20). Resolutions of fact or value may deal with past, present, or future events and relationships. Here are some examples of parliamentary debate resolutions of fact or value:

- *This House believes that the media limit the marketplace of ideas.*
- *This House believes that integration has failed.*
- *This House recognizes that the United Nations will disappear.*
- *This House believes that pornography damages women.*
- *This House believes that libertarianism is inadequate.*

Notice that none of these resolutions demands any type of action step. Although you may respond by thinking of several possible action steps, the resolution's construction does not require you to advocate one in the debate. Thus we have a key distinction between fact, value and policy resolutions in parliamentary debate. Recognizing this distinction is a first step in constructing your overall strategic approach to the debate.

We remind you once again: when supporting resolutions of fact or value, develop a case that limits your burden of proof. Perhaps the most consistent mistake beginning debate teams make when debating the Government side of the resolution is taking on a larger burden than the resolution requires. Ask yourselves, "What does the resolution require that we prove?" Then ask, "What does the resolution *not* require that we prove?"

In our example of media limiting the marketplace of ideas, the resolution requires the Government to show that the media do somehow limit the marketplace of ideas. In contrast, the Government does not need to show that the media conspire to do so or that the media are the sole cause of a limited marketplace of ideas or even that the limitation on the marketplace of ideas is a bad thing. Nothing in the wording of the resolution requires the Government to illustrate anything beyond the declaration that the media limit the marketplace of ideas.

DEVELOPING FACT AND VALUE CASES

Once you and your partner have determined what your basic burdens are, it is time to set up a case supporting the resolution. All resolutions of fact or value—indeed, all resolutions in parliamentary debate—necessitate a definition of terms as discussed in Chapter Eight. It will be the Prime Minister's responsibility to carefully identify the nature of the fact or value being considered before the House. The Prime Minister traditionally defines the key terms in the resolution in the first few minutes of the constructive speech. Using the media example, it is undoubtedly important for the Government team to identify what it means by "media," "limits," and "marketplace of ideas." These **key terms** in the resolution need clarification to foster a more intelligible debate.

Following the definition of these terms, you and your partner must develop the existence of the fact or value statement as presented by applying the definitions to a particular circumstance. Let's say you have chosen to define the terms in the following manner:

- *Media* refers primarily to television.
- *Marketplace of ideas* represents the issues, theories, and concerns of the American electorate during presidential elections.
- *Limited* means narrowed and restricted.

Given these definitions, it might be that your particular circumstance involves the televised presidential debates. In other words, the televised presidential debates would be your specific illustration supporting the contention that the media limit the marketplace of ideas.

Once you have defined the key terms and set out the particular case by which to examine the resolution, you are prepared to illustrate that special circumstances do not prevent us from accepting the fact or value claim. To inoculate your case against arguments that the particular circumstance presented (the televised presidential debates) does not provide sufficient proof for the case presented, the Prime Minister should advance arguments preventing anticipated attacks from your opponent. The need for such inoculating arguments creates the challenge of trying to put yourselves in your opponents' shoes and anticipating their objections. Though not a simple task, it is a necessary strategic move.

To recap, one overall strategic approach to developing cases to support resolutions of fact or value involves defining the terms, applying the definition to a particular circumstance, and showing that special circumstances do not prevent us from accepting the fact or value claim.

A second approach to developing a case to support a fact or value claim involves a greater focus on the criteria put forth to justify the fact or value judgment. **Criteria** can be defined as the standards by which a decision is made. If you and your friend have a debate about the best movie of the 1990s, it would be important to establish the criteria or standards by which the term *best* should be applied. If your friend believes box office sales signifies the best film but you believe critical acclaim is the most important element for judgment, chances are quite good that the two of you will argue in circles. Establishing agreed-on criteria for decision making seeks to prevent this type of situation.

In establishing criteria, the Government team presents arguments for the criteria or standards it believes should be applied. Continuing with the example of the best movie of the 1990s, the Government team would put forth criteria useful in judging which film indeed deserves the label *best*. The advocate might claim that the judgment should be based on originality, cinematography, and acting when deciding which movie was the best. These three elements would represent the specific standards by which a proper judgment of a movie's worth would be made.

The next step is to illustrate the relevance of the criteria to the nature of the judgment expressed in the resolution. In short, the advocate must justify the use of the criteria presented. You must answer the question, "Why should those three elements be considered when deciding which film is the best?"

Once the character and the relevance of the criteria have been presented, the facts of the specific circumstances under consideration are analyzed using those same criteria. For example, the Government might assert that *Titanic* was the best film of the 1990s because it met the three proposed criteria: It was original, it had excellent cinematography, and the acting was superb. In this type of debate, the bulk of the argumentation in the round centers on the justification of the use of the criteria rather than the specific application of the proposed standards. In the aforementioned example, the argumentation would focus on the employment of originality, cinematography, and acting as standards by which to pass judgment on a film.

Finally, in what is arguably the most common fact or value case form in parliamentary debate, the focus of the debate is the application of **implicit criteria**. The setup for this type of case dispenses with a direct justification of the criteria. Rather, this type of case assumes that the criteria are readily accepted or understood by those present and the case centers on demonstrating that the facts of the situation conform to the criteria.

For example, in the proposition *This House believes that integration has failed*, the Government team assumes that the state of race relations and the socioeconomic status of people of color are relevant criteria by which to judge the success or failure of integration. The focus of the Government case is to prove that integration has failed, not that using the standards of the state of race relations and socioeconomic status of people of color are legitimate standards by which to measure integration. Although this does not mean the Opposition will ignore your choice of criteria, it does mean your strategic choice is to place the focus on the application of those criteria.

To prove the case using the implicit criteria form, the Government might establish claims that argue that hate crimes against people of color are rampant. In addition, the Government might argue that people of color are still underrepresented in the management of corporate America. In this case, the issue is whether these specific issues, hate crimes and corporate management, meet the criteria to establish that integration has failed.

OPPOSITION APPROACHES TO FACT AND VALUE

So far we have discussed three strategic Government approaches for fact or value resolutions in parliamentary debate. Here we discuss three case strategies for Opposition teams when faced with a fact or value resolution:

- Attacking the Government definition or criteria
- Rejection of the Government application of the definition or criteria
- Demonstration of the superiority of the Opposition value system

One strategy for an Opposition team approaching a fact or value resolution consists of attacking the criteria advanced by the Government. Quite simply, the Opposition argues that the standards by which the Government has chosen to analyze the object in question are faulty.

Let us use the resolution *This House believes that pornography damages women*. Should the Government define *pornography* as "any symbolic representation of women engaged in nonconsensual sexual acts," and *damage* as "action that promotes physical endangerment or harm," the Opposition strategy of attacking the definitions or criteria might consist of attacking the Government's definition of pornography. Perhaps the Opposition might ask how the Government would prove the sexual acts in question were nonconsensual. In addition, the Opposition might reject the definitions as overly broad. The Opposition might also ask how the Government team would illustrate that other cultural factors, such as the availability of weapons, poverty, and symbolic representations of violence that are without sexual content, could be discounted as factors contributing to violence against women.

Should the audience accept your Opposition attack against the definition or criteria put forth by the Government team, that would most likely lead to a complete defeat of the resolution and an Opposition victory. This direct approach should be used only when the Government criteria are illogical and unacceptable. To argue that the Government criteria are inappropriate when it is obvious that they are appropriate would only serve to make you appear foolish—not a favored strategy for winning a debate.

A second strategy for an Opposition team seeking to defeat a fact or value resolution involves critiquing the application of the criteria identified by the Government team. This approach accepts the Government definitions and criteria yet claims it has been misused in the Government case. For example, let us examine the resolution *This House believes class is more important than race in America*. As written, this is clearly a nonpolicy resolution. There is no explicit call for action. Suppose the Government defines all of the key terms to your satisfaction but goes on to claim that the unacceptably low number of representatives in Congress coming from low-income households illustrates that class is indeed more important than race. You, on the Opposition, might well agree that such a disparity exists but contend that to separate economic status from racial and ethnic makeup inaccurately portrays the reality. The Opposition rejects the specific application of the criteria in the instance identified, thereby defeating the Government case.

One more tactic for opposing fact or value resolutions involves demonstrating the superiority of the Opposition value system. Rather than arguing at the level of definitions or criteria, the Opposition seeks to illustrate the erroneous prioritizing and judgment of the Government team.

Take the example of the resolution *This House believes that might makes right*. Suppose the Government team linked this resolution to a case claiming that United States military action was justified in response to Iraqi actions in the Persian Gulf region in the early 1990s. An Opposition team choosing to employ the value superiority position might press the preeminence of a foreign policy based on diplomacy and peace. The Opposition might argue that the results of the U.S. decision to use military might has resulted in the deaths of thousands of innocent citizens, the continuation of Saddam Hussein's dictatorship, and untold damage to the environment. The Opposition might then go on to argue the broader benefits of diplomacy and peace rather than militaristic approaches to discord.

CONCLUSION

In this chapter, we have attempted to outline methods that both the Government and the Opposition can use to approach propositions of fact and value. We assert that these types of resolutions are inherently linked, and so we have demonstrated how to treat the elements of fact and value cases. Understanding fact and value resolutions and how to approach building these cases is necessary for a successful parliamentary debate career.

Chapter Ten

⎯⎯⎯⎯ ⧉⧉⧉ ⎯⎯⎯⎯

Policy Resolutions

Key Concepts

Agency—the ability to implement the solution to a problem

Alternative solution—an Opposition strategy involving suggesting a different plan

Blame—the determination of who is at fault

Cure—the solution to the problem

Defense of the status quo—an Opposition strategy of arguing in favor of the current system

Ill—the problem to be solved

Inherency—the requirement to prove that the problem stems from the system in question

Significance—proof that a problem matters

- 🕊 *This House would privatize social security.*
- 🕊 *This House would support mandatory community service.*
- 🕊 *This House should legalize it.*

Although the subject matter in these three resolutions is decidedly different, they do have one element in common: their explicit reference to some type of action. Resolutions in parliamentary debate indicating a course of action are known as *policy resolutions*. To achieve success in parliamentary debate, you will need to understand the ins and outs of debating resolutions of policy. Accordingly, in this chapter we focus our discussion on supporting and defeating resolutions of policy.

Initially, the task of supporting a plan of action in a parliamentary debate may appear quite daunting. Parliamentary debate requires you to construct a case in fifteen minutes. Nevertheless, with time and effort you will find yourself able to devise a coherent case worthy of support. Our aim here is to assist you in that process.

CREATING GOVERNMENT POLICY CASES

In the belief that a concrete example will make plain the general principles in our discussion, we will use the following resolution: *This House would abolish grades in higher education.* Clearly this resolution advocates a course of action. A conventional interpretation of the resolution would have the Government urging support for the elimination of grades in our system of higher education. However, be certain that before diving into the gritty details of case construction, you and your partner agree on the general meaning of the resolution. Although it may seem obvious to you that the elimination of letter grades at the college level is what the resolution is about, your partner might be thinking about tenure or some other aspect of higher education. Avoid wasting precious time working toward different goals by confirming your interpretation of the resolution with your partner, and keep in mind that some policy resolutions are more directive and explicit than others.

Once you and your partner have a general agreement as to the resolution's meaning, decide on the most basic burdens the resolution requires. What does the resolution ask you to prove or not prove? Once you have a finger on the rudimentary burdens the resolution requires of both you and your opponents, it is time to consider your strategic approach.

Argumentation and debate theorists have identified several issues advocates need to address to argue comprehensively for a specific plan of action. Some disagreement exists concerning the exact number and definitive terms for these stock issues (so called because they are fundamental or basic to policy debate); however, we can be sure that advocates for a plan of action need to address the basic areas of ill, blame, cure, agency, and cost within their plan. It is imperative that you firmly grasp these rudimentary concepts for policy debate, so we will attempt to explain them clearly and concisely.

Ill

You are undoubtedly familiar with the old saw, "If it ain't broke, don't fix it." And you have probably also heard the saying that someone has "created a solution in search of a problem." Both clichés call to mind the need for policy advocates to specify the problem before proposing a solution. This is the stock issue of **ill**. Quite simply, you must answer the question, "What's wrong?" You and your partner need to identify and describe the nature of the ill before launching into your plan. In the case of our example, to abolish grades, it is not good enough simply to assert that a problem exists in our nation's colleges and universities. You must convince your audience that this problem matters; that it is significant. Before getting a fair hearing from your audience about your proposed solution, it is vital to create a sense of urgency by establishing the significance of the ill you have identified. If your audience is not convinced that the problem is important to them, you will have great difficulty convincing them to consider your solution.

How do you address the issue of significance? Look to the people in your audience. What do you think they care about? Which issues concerning higher education and grades will create a sense of urgency? What do these people value? What damage is being done to those values?

Many experts suggest a two-pronged approach whereby you illustrate significance both quantitatively and qualitatively. A quantitative approach articulates the large numbers or high percentage of people touched or influenced by the problem. In the example concerning education and grades, you might point to the overwhelming percentage of colleges and universities employing a system in which grades demarcate performance and effort. Furthermore, you might cite the increasing numbers of people attending institutions of higher education. The specific numbers are less important than the undeniable claim that large numbers of students are subject to such a system and have suffered harm.

Another tactic, often capable of eliciting a more emotional response, involves a qualitative method of support. Rather than addressing how many, a qualitative approach focuses on "in what ways" and "to what degree." Here we have a discussion at the micro level of the problem.

Continuing with the instance concerning the abolishment of grades, a qualitative example might center on one person's experience and explore the severity and degree of damage done to this single, representative example. If you were arguing that a system of grades creates an intensely competitive environment that is hostile to teamwork and learning, you might launch into a narrative of how one student suffered directly from this system. A qualitative focus often increases the sense of identification an audience has with a problem and its attendant consequences. A combination of both quantitative and qualitative examples can provide powerful support in establishing the **significance** of the problem you and your partner seek to address.

Blame

Once you have established the ill and the degree of significance, it becomes necessary to address the stock issue of **blame**. Who or what is at fault? Who or what causes the problem (the ill) that has been identified? Let's go back to our example concerning the abolishment of grades. You must demonstrate that the system of grades is responsible for the ill you have identified. Your opponent will most likely attempt to shift the blame for the ill to another causal factor. To prevent this, you need to address the stock issue of blame by convincing your audience that the blame lies with the grading system. Unless you convince the audience that the system is to blame, argumentation referring to abolishment of the system will be worthless. This leads to the concept of *inherency*.

Inherency refers to the necessity for you, the advocate of the plan, to show that the problem results from the system as it is, the status quo, and therefore that it is necessary to implement change to properly address the ill or problem. You must illustrate that the ill is inherent in the present system. Let's simplify this using our education example.

To successfully advocate the policy of abolishing grades, you and your partner need to demonstrate that fundamental to causing the ills you have identified is the existence of the grading system. You must establish that there is something essential to the grading system and its relationship to students that create severe problems demanding our attention. You must prevent your opponents from successfully arguing that other factors are primarily responsible for the problems mentioned in the debate. If your opponents can convince the judge that fixing the system will not solve the problem, you have lost the stock issue of inherency.

Apart from addressing the stock issues that focus on the cause and magnitude of a particular problem, you and your partner may propose a solution to that same problem. Your decision to propose a solution should be a carefully considered strategic decision based on your analysis of the entire rhetorical situation. The following are two important questions to consider when developing a policy case:

- Does the resolution require a proposal to address the problem?
- Can we successfully support the resolution without proposing a plan to solve the problem?

Cure

Should you reach the conclusion that you will propose a plan to address the problem, you will broach the stock issue of **cure**. As its label implies, this stock issue concerns the method or plan for addressing the ill or problem. Now that we understand the problem and its urgency, what should be done about it?

Once you have decided to propose a plan of action, you must consider the degree of specificity you will offer. It is vital to keep in mind that as you increase the scope and specificity of your proposal for solving the problem, you also increase the target your opponents can attack. Furthermore, since you typically have only fifteen minutes in which to construct your case, most audiences will not expect a comprehensive proposal addressing every single contingency.

Agency

The stock issue of **agency** centers on the question, "Who will be responsible for implementing and monitoring the plan?" If your plan calls for using portfolios instead of letter grades, you should be prepared to explain what person or group will be responsible for the plan. In other words, will it be the individual school districts who will decide how portfolios will be produced and critiqued? Or will it be a national program under the auspices of the federal Department of Education? In another example, a team proposing a plan to address the problems of the homeless population will need to explain which agency or group will be responsible for the policy. Simply asserting that we should spend more money to help the homeless will not win you many debate rounds. You will need to identify in your case, or at least be prepared to respond to a question from your Opposition concerning agency, to improve your chances of successfully persuading the House to adopt the plan.

Cost

Finally, if you decide to propose some sort of plan, you and your partner will almost inevitably encounter the stock issue of **cost**. Living in a capitalistic society, you are no doubt familiar with the concept of cost as it relates to money. However, the stock issue of cost may also refer to expenses that transcend money. How will the current system be disrupted? How much time will this take away from other activities? Might the proposal affect other elements related to the system and, if so, how? Apart from strictly monetary costs, the stock issue of cost can refer to social costs, psychological costs, opportunity costs, and any number of other expenses incurred when implementing the plan.

If we apply the stock issue of cost to the education resolution, we might discover that there are costs involved with teachers' time if we move to a portfolio system since portfolios take a great deal of time to evaluate. Consequently, a Government team proposing a portfolio plan must account for the time expenditure in its original case or be prepared to address it should the Opposition cite this cost in its own case.

OPPOSITION STRATEGIES

Now that you are familiar with the stock issues of ill, blame, cure, agency, and cost, let's look at four strategies for opposing resolutions of policy in parliamentary debate:

- Defense of the status quo
- Repair of the present system
- Direct refutation of case
- Alternative solution

Your analysis of the specifics of the debate should dictate which approach, or combination of approaches, you will take.

A **defense of the status quo** is a defense of the current system. In the example of the resolution *This House would abolish grades in higher education,* in opposing the Government case you would seek to illustrate the strengths and advantages of the present system of using grades at our colleges and universities. It is not necessary to argue that the present system is perfect, only that in light of the present circumstances and in comparison to the Government's proposal, it is the superior course of action.

One advantage of supporting the status quo is that you should have the advantage of presumption on your side. As noted in Chapter Seven, presumption is the inherent advantage in opposing change (Ziegelmueller and Kay 24). Although the judge's ballot asks the question, "Which team did the better debating?" all things being equal, advocates need to show a compelling reason to change. Absent a compelling reason to change policies, there is no reason to seek change, and more often than not, the Opposition will win the debate by supporting the status quo.

Nevertheless, keep in mind that some advocates of parliamentary debate believe that this type of debate demands a different perspective on presumption. Some have argued that because debaters on both sides have only fifteen minutes of preparation time, it is unfair to penalize the Government team by accepting Opposition presumption. In this case, neutral presumption exists, or the idea that the team advocating change need not have a greater burden of proof. Therefore, it is wise to keep in mind that simply refuting the policy supported by the Government may not be enough to win the debate. A strong Opposition team will also put forth strong reasons why the status quo does not require change. By upholding the status quo with strong arguments in addition to illustrating the disadvantages and problems with the Government case, you will enhance your possibility of winning the debate.

A second basic Opposition strategy against a Government team supporting a policy resolution entails advocating a repair of the present system. This strategy requires a continued commitment to the underlying tenets of the present policy approach but recognizes the desirability of minor changes for improvement. Rather than tearing down the house and building anew, this approach involves changes in the existing structure. Should you choose the strategy of minor changes, be certain to avoid going too far in criticizing the present system lest you end up supporting the Government team's arguments. An Opposition team advocating minor repairs needs to make clear its continued support of the fundamental principles of present policies and its dissimilarity to the Government's approach.

Take the example of the resolution *This House supports significant restrictions on private ownership of firearms.* In opposing this policy resolution, you might advocate increased availability and incentives for firearms education and training. This minor repairs approach would endorse a change in existing policy (greater access and encouragement for firearms education) yet would maintain opposition to significant changes in existing laws concerning firearms.

This position would oppose any major changes advocated by the Government while arguing for the underlying philosophy of the less restrictive approach of the current policy. Central to any effective minor repairs approach would be quality argumentation illustrating the philosophical tenets supporting the status quo. Tell the judge how and why justice, liberty, equality, and pragmatism are better supported by the current approach with a few minor repairs. This Opposition approach can prove successful but must be utilized carefully. You and your partner must be certain to avoid advocating changes in the existing policy which support the resolution or are inconsistent with the philosophical approach underlying the current system.

A third tactic for an Opposition team combating a resolution of policy is that of straight refutation. In our view, this approach is most appropriate in response to a poorly conceived Government policy. With this method, commitment to support the status quo is unnecessary. You may refer to the current system in your argumentation, but your overriding focus remains countering the Government's plan. The straight refutation approach is risky, however, and runs counter to the belief that Opposition teams must build up in addition to tear down. Still, a major advantage of this strategy is that you need not burden yourself with the responsibility of defending current practices or any particular policy.

You might find this approach useful should you have very limited knowledge of the topic at hand. If you have a firm grasp on the fundamentals of reasoning and argumentation, you should have little problem attacking the logic underlying the Government's position. Furthermore, if you limit this approach to situations where the Government advocates a poorly conceived case, you should find this strategy sufficient.

A final, and perhaps most controversial Opposition strategy, would be advocating an **alternative solution**—a competing policy proposal. Here the Opposition admits that a serious problem or defect exists in the status quo but counters the Government's advocacy with its own plan to address the problems identified by both teams. The Opposition does not attempt to defend the status quo.

Should you choose to employ this Opposition strategy, you would offer a plan of action that is distinct from the proposal suggested in the resolution or advocated by the Government team. In addition, the plan must compete directly with the Government proposal and be argued as mutually exclusive as well. In other words, it would be either impractical or structurally impossible for both plans to be implemented at the same time.

An example will illustrate this strategy: *This House would operate on the health care system.* The Government advocates complete privatization of health care. The Opposition argues for a government-run, single-payer system. Health care cannot be private and government-run at the same time.

CONCLUSION

In this chapter, we have discussed supporting and opposing resolutions of policy. We have looked at the stock issues for policy resolutions and have provided examples illustrating their basic characteristics. This chapter is by no means a comprehensive treatise on debates; it is merely a beginning to the conversation. Still, a firm grasp of these basic issues for policy resolutions is a must for any successful parliamentary debater.

Chapter Eleven

Refutation and Rebuttal in Constructive Speeches

Key Concepts

Rebuttal—reinforcing arguments
Refutation—attacking directly asserted arguments

Both teams in a debate attempt to construct a case to prove their side of the argument. Yet in so doing, they must also try to attack the other team's case so that in the end the only case remaining is their own. This parrying back and forth is known as **refutation** and **rebuttal**. Refutation and rebuttal are much like building and tearing down a house; you keep trying to knock down the foundation pillars while the other team tries to rebuild. In this chapter, we will give you strategies for undermining the pillars of your opponent's case and for rebuilding the pillars of your own.

Knowing how to build a case, as we have discussed in earlier chapters, provides you with the elements for tearing down a case. We will begin with refutation by looking at evidence, then consider reasoning, and finally look at the claim itself and its impact on the entire case. Then we will turn our attention to rebuttal.

EVIDENCE

A claim is only as strong as the evidence that supports it; without evidence, a claim is merely an assertion. Therefore, attacking evidence is a key way to begin refuting a case. In parliamentary debate, evidence is most often of the example type. So to refute an argument, you must analyze what the example attempts to tell the audience.

Examples

There are several questions that you must ask yourself to test the validity of an example.

Does the example support the claim? Suppose that the claim is that politicians are corrupt. The Government team supports this claim by using the example of Senator Robert Packwood and his sexual indiscretions. Though there is little doubt that his extracurricular activities were reprehensible, as the Opposition you must ask yourself whether sexual misconduct equals corruption.

Is the example representative of the whole? In our example, if the Government team cites Richard Nixon and the Watergate scandal as evidence, you must ask whether Nixon's actions are representative of all politicians'. If you do not believe that this is the case, you must provide sufficient examples where it is not the case.

Is the example explained sufficiently? When giving an example, a team may be tempted to leave out significant details. In discussing corrupt politicians, a team might cite Bill Clinton and the Whitewater scandal. At first glance, this would seem to illustrate Clinton's corruption. However, a savvy Opposition team would readily point out that though Clinton was linked to the scandal, he was not convicted of any wrongdoing.

These three questions will go far in uncovering potential flaws in evidence by example.

Analogy

Another commonly used form of evidence is the analogy, saying that what is true in one case will probably be true in the other. Like evidence by example, evidence by analogy can be examined by answering questions about the analogy.

Are the two cases similar enough to be compared? Suppose the team argued that Watergate forced Nixon to resign; therefore, Whitewater should do the same for Clinton. In contrast, the opposing team need only point out that Watergate involved illegal activity while Nixon was president and the illegal activity was political in nature. Further, evidence proved Nixon's involvement. For Clinton, Whitewater occurred prior to his presidency, was not political, and has yielded no evidence of wrongdoing. Therefore, the cases are not comparable enough to warrant drawing similar conclusions.

Are there extenuating circumstances that render the conclusion problematic? For example, in a debate on public education, one team could contend that given the faltering public school system, a solution might be a free market approach. The team could suggest that since this path has proven successful in the computer industry, applying a free market philosophy to the educational system would reap the same rewards. Upon closer examination, we discover that though education and the computer industry are interested in outcomes and improvement, the computer industry produces mainly homogeneous products to be sold. Education, by contrast, challenges individuals to reach their unique potential. The philosophical differences make the comparison ineffective.

Statistics

When a team uses statistics in parliamentary debate, they can pose problems for the opposing team since carded evidence is not permitted in the round. Consequently, the opposing team must ask two questions about the statistics:

Are the statistics well known? A team could reasonable cite that roughly half of all marriages in the United States end in divorce, as most people have heard this statistic. But if a team states that 62 percent of all married couples cheat (a fictional number), the judge would be less inclined to accept this number as fact because it is not common knowledge. In such cases, the opposing team should ask for the source of this information. Even if the reply is that it was broadcast on *20/20*, the questioning can still raise doubts in the mind of the judge.

Are the statistics reasonable? Because of the nature of parliamentary debate, teams can be tempted to fabricate numbers to support their case. This should *never* happen. It is unethical. When you listen to a statistic, think about whether the statistic is reasonable. Could it be true? Suppose a debater in a moment of panic threw out the statistic that 34 percent of Americans die of AIDS. Clearly, the statistic is not reasonable, and therefore both the claim and the ethics of the debater can be called into question.

Authority

Evidence from authority should undergo similar questioning. Most often teams will cite philosophers or well-known theorists to support positions in a team's case. Thorough knowledge of common ideas of philosophers and general theories as discussed in the research chapter of this text (see Chapter Four) will allow you to look at the basic content of the opposing team's argument to test the veracity of its claims. Interesting debates often ensue that deal with interpretations of philosophical assumptions or theoretical constructs. Whatever the case, examining the content of the claim is often the best place to start.

Of equal importance is to look at the authorities themselves. Asking questions about the authorities often provides ample ammunition for refutation.

Is the authority an expert on the topic at hand? A person may have a list of credentials a mile long, but unless they have expertise in the field of discussion, their credentials may be worthless. One example of misplaced authority that springs to mind occurs every four years during presidential elections. Hollywood celebrities will often promote a particular candidate and appear in commercials expressing that support. The public is supposed to attach credibility to the candidate based on the claims of a celebrity, though clearly, the celebrity probably has little personal expertise in the field of politics.

Is this the authority's current or most recent view on the topic? As humans, we are prone to learn and reevaluate our view of the world and the issues that surface in that world. Politicians are especially susceptible to such mental meanderings. As an opposing team, you should be sure to question whether the authority cited still supports the purported view. An example would be citing Clinton's campaign promise to associate most favored nation trading status with human rights. However, since being elected, Clinton has advocated renewal of most favored nation trading status with China, a known human rights violator. Aware teams stay abreast of the changing political and philosophical landscapes that often enter into debates.

Any use of evidence requires the opposing team to scrutinize the evidence to make sure that it supports the claim. A team can attack the validity of the evidence by pointing out weaknesses in the evidence. In addition, the opposing team can provide counterevidence that disproves the claim. So if Team A cites Watergate as an example of the corruption of politicians, Team B might offer Senator Mark Hatfield as an example of an honest politician. Opposing teams do best by both tearing down evidence and offering competing evidence.

REASONING

If reasoning is the link between evidence and claim, then we are justified to assume that attacking the reasoning is a valuable place to continue the assault on a case. As we discussed in the chapter on fallacies (see Chapter Five), faults in reasoning disable a claim.

CLAIM

A good case structure will include claims as general propositions that a team hopes to prove as true. A skilled opposing team will consider the claim's truthfulness and its relationship to the entire case. However, the fact that there is nothing obviously wrong with either the evidence or the reasoning does not mean that the claim cannot be refuted. You can still argue that either the claim does not support the resolution or that the impact of the claim is insignificant in helping the opposing team's case. For example, consider the resolution *This House would legalize prostitution* and the Government claims that prostitution increases the incidence of sexually transmitted diseases. The Government's evidence and reasoning support this claim. To counter this, the Opposition would agree and point out that it is indeed true *in a system where prostitution is unregulated*. The Opposition has appropriated the Government's claim to strengthen its own case. Any time a team offers a claim, you should consider exactly what the claim attempts to prove and the impact that the claim has for the case.

REBUTTAL

Refutation requires that you consider how the arguments are put together and how the individual arguments support the resolution. Once your case has been the subject of refutation, you should then turn your attention to rebutting your own case. Suppose a team has seemingly destroyed your partner's evidence, reasoning, and claims. Instead of throwing in the towel, you must rebut your case using a three-step process: link, lead, and load. These steps reflect the three basic methods of refutation.

First, you should *link* the claim to the resolution, explaining how the claim supports your position in terms of the resolution. If the opposing team has argued that guns killing people supports their case that the pen is mightier than the sword, you can link this claim to the fact that the pen can help to curb these killings and therefore the pen is mightier than the sword.

Next, *lead* the judge through the reasoning again. If the opposing team has argued that your reasoning is faulty because you have used a hasty generalization, you can show the judge why drawing conclusions from your evidence is justified based on the available cases.

Finally, you can *load* your original claim with even more evidence. When you are preparing a case, try to make sure that each partner has examples or statistics to support a resolution so that the second speaker has new information to extend the claim. This makes the case even stronger and more difficult for the other team to refute again. Using these strategies will give you a starting point for rebuilding your case.

CONCLUSION

This chapter is aimed at giving you basic strategies for refuting and rebutting cases. We cannot claim that this is an exhaustive list for ways to attack a case. For example, one could clearly attack the qualifier in a claim. If a team suggested that "some guns are justified" without expounding on what was meant, you could attack the idea of what "some" means. However, for our purposes, the minimum that you must attack is the evidence, reasoning, and claim. When you have mastered these points of refutation, other elements will come easily.

Chapter Twelve

Rebuttal Speeches

Key Concepts

Clarify—to reiterate controversial points
Condense—to reiterate the main points of a case
Crystallize—to limit arguments to the winning points
Voting issues—the key points in a debate that are pivotal to
    the outcome

Each side in a parliamentary debate delivers one rebuttal speech. The
Opposition's speech is four minutes and the Government's speech is five minutes. While it is tempting for both teams to simply rehash the arguments that
have been presented in the round, a better strategy is to crystallize, clarify, and
condense. Rebuttals fare much like closing arguments in a trial. It is your opportunity to tell your narrative of how the round evolved. You can persuade the
audience by offering a perspective on how to view the arguments and refutation presented in the round. You will find that many a round is won or lost in
rebuttals. We will discuss the strategies for rebuttal in this chapter.

CRYSTALLIZE

Instead of repeating the entire case and reiterating every argument, explaining
why you have won that particular argument, the first strategy of rebuttal is to

crystallize your winning points. This means to pick three or four elements of your case that should be voting issues for the audience. **Voting issues** are the salient points in the debate that you believe should determine the outcome of the debate. Suppose your value as presented in the Prime Minister's constructive was national sovereignty. If one of your voting issues is the value, you could explain how you have upheld national sovereignty with your case. Here you might take an example from your first point, the extension your partner gave on the second point, and the reasoning of the third point to illustrate how your case supports national sovereignty.

Crystallizing the salient issues communicates to the audience what you view as the most important points in the debate. In this way, they are given a perspective from which to view the opposing arguments presented in the debate. Crystallizing requires that you draw on all arguments in the round to show how your team is winning the debate.

CLARIFY

When you **clarify** in rebuttal, it enables you to explain for the final time your side's position on the arguments that have developed in the debate. Suppose the resolution stated *This House would reform campaign finances* and during the debate your team argued that you would limit soft money. If your definition has been a point of contention in the round, the rebuttal is your last opportunity to make sure that the audience understands your position exactly.

You can also clarify what the opposing team has argued in the debate. If the opposing team has offered arguments that are contradictory or fall outside the realm of the resolution, you can clarify these points for the audience, in effect preempting any further argumentation on this point.

CONDENSE

As we have stated, the last thing an audience wants to hear in rebuttal is the same arguments rehashed in the same manner. Nevertheless, you do need to make sure that you are hitting the main points of the case in the rebuttal; therefore, you must **condense** them. You might argue that the definitional debate really comes down to the meaning of the word *substantial*. Instead of repeating what both sides have said, simply offer the definition that should be accepted along with compelling reasons to accept that definition. Condensing arguments is necessary in order to crystallize the elements of the debate in the limited time frame offered for rebuttals. You need not restate all the arguments; stick to the basics.

STYLE

Rebuttals are your final opportunity to convince the audience to accept your case and argumentation. This is where you give the audience reasons to vote for you. It is also your last opportunity to leave a lasting impression on the audience. So you should remember to begin with the introductions and then tell the audience the three or four points that you think will win the debate for your team.

Regardless of how you think the debate is going, you should remember that rebuttal puts a new spin on what has already been heard. Although you cannot make a new argument, you can tell the audience what the earlier arguments mean. Many times, you may feel that there is no way that you can win a debate. However, you never know what the audience is thinking. So you need to put your best foot forward. Never concede a debate in rebuttals. If you think you have lost a major argument, minimize its importance in your rebuttal and focus on the arguments that you know you are winning and show why those are the important arguments on which the debate should be decided.

CONCLUSION

Rebuttals are important speeches in the debate. Though new information cannot be presented, a new way of looking at the cases can be. Teams should spend time developing their rebuttal skills since these speeches can make or break a round. We have shown you how to crystallize, clarify, and condense. In addition, we have offered some stylistic pointers that should help you to present a great rebuttal.

Part III

Elements of the Round

Chapter Thirteen

Preparation Time

Key Concepts

Case statement—a team's basic approach to and
   interpretation of the resolution
Opposition philosophy—the approach the Opposition will
   take toward the resolution and the Government case
Resolutional burdens—the responsibility of each team as
   defined by the resolution

This House would exterminate capital punishment; you have fifteen minutes—that's only nine hundred seconds—about the time it takes *MTV* to show 14,000 commercials—for you and your partner to prepare for the round. What should be done during the fifteen-minute prep time? How can you use this time efficiently? This chapter will focus on the fifteen minutes parliamentary debaters have between the reading of the resolution and the beginning of the debate.

Some people use prep time to complain about the previous debate, gulp down a latte, and talk about posttournament activities. These are the same people sitting in the audience during the final debate. Though efficient use of the preparation period will not guarantee success, failing to use it efficiently can indeed make the difference between winning and losing. We will focus here on the basics. Each team will develop its own idiosyncratic methods.

Although a great deal of overlap exists between prepping as the Government team and doing so as the Opposition, for clarity we will focus first on Government team preparation and follow it with a focus on prepping as the Opposition.

GOVERNMENT PREP TIME

You and your partner are representing the Government team on the resolution *This House would exterminate capital punishment.* For most debaters, this is a fairly straightforward resolution. Most judges will come into the debate expecting that you and your partner will propose ending the practice of executing human beings convicted of capital offenses. Of course, some teams might choose to put a twist on this, perhaps by defining capital punishment as the practice of ending the lives of animals in laboratory research. Teams choosing such creative links are taking a substantial risk and must be prepared to tell a convincing narrative that links the case to the resolution.

Following the reading of the resolution, many Government teams choose to stay in the room while the Opposition team leaves to discuss its case. We strongly suggest that both teams prepare out of earshot of the adjudicator for the debate. Do your best to find a place with a minimum of distractions. With only fifteen minutes, there is no time to waste.

The first question to ponder is, "What does the resolution require we prove?" The first minute of prep should focus on answering this question. Remember, as the Government team, you want to avoid putting more of a burden on yourselves than the resolution necessitates. Study the resolution's language carefully. If any words in the resolution are unfamiliar or ambiguous, this is where your pocket dictionary may be useful. A cursory glance in any dictionary would indicate that the term *exterminate* means to get rid of completely. Therefore, at the most basic level, the resolution requires that you as the Government prove that capital punishment, the death penalty, needs to be eliminated or ended. This should take no more than one minute of prep time.

Once you have established the minimal burden of the resolution by answering the question about what the resolution requires, the next question to address is, "What does the resolution *not* require that we prove?" This question serves to aid you and your partner by limiting your burden. Again, you want to avoid placing a larger burden of proof on yourselves than the resolution requires, and answering the second question should assist in that process. Furthermore, this serves to alert you to additional burdens the Opposition might seek to place on you and your partner once the debate begins.

In our sample resolution, the answer to the second question might be that the resolution does not require us to specify exactly how and when capital punishment will be abolished. During the initial minutes of prep time, it is imperative that you firmly establish the specific burdens and central goal of your argumentation. If you are fuzzy and unclear of the purpose of your case, you will have great difficulty constructing it. To use an overemployed metaphor, the first few minutes of prep should establish the blueprints of your case. Ideally, answering the second question will take no longer than one minute as well.

After engaging in resolutional analysis and establishing what the resolution does and does not require that you prove, the next part of your prep time should be spent focusing on general proof of the resolution. This third step is to secure your case thesis, or what is sometimes referred to as your case statement. This is what you intend to support in your argumentation. We cannot emphasize enough how important it is to have the case statement or thesis firmly established in your minds. You and your partner are already facing a challenge in debating another two-person team. Do not increase the difficulty by working at cross-purposes with your own partner!

Next, you need to take the time to specify the language of your case statement. It is not good enough to have a rough idea of what you are doing. Not establishing the specific word choice of your case statement during prep time will leave you vulnerable in the debate. Continuing our example, the case statement might be "Capital punishment must be eliminated in the United States." Not all case statements will be as simple as this, but you and your partner should spend no longer than two minutes crafting the specific language. This is also the time to develop your definitions that lead into the case statement. (Defining terms was discussed in Chapter Eight.)

So far we have used four minutes of prep time. We have engaged in resolutional analysis and crafted our case statement. The fourth step is to focus on proving the thesis. This will necessarily take into account the type of resolution you are defending (refer to Chapter Six, on Government case construction, for the specifics.) During this part of your prep time, you and your partner need to negotiate your rhetorical strategy for supporting the resolution. This will most likely prove the lengthiest part of your preparation.

This fourth step should be devoted to the major arguments you are going to use to support the thesis. There are several ways of approaching this, but the end result should be a cohesive plan. Far too many teams enter the debate with a vague idea of how they plan to support their case, and some end up with one partner contradicting the other partner's arguments. You might choose to simply throw out different arguments and discuss them as they come up. Some teams prefer to write down a short list of positions individually for a minute or so and then discuss what they have developed. Both methods have advantages and disadvantages. You and your partner should experiment during practice debates to see which works best for you.

Regardless of your specific method, this part of prep time should result in a list of major arguments to support your case statement. The two of you need to agree on the ordering of the arguments, and your plan should include independent lines of argument that the second speaker will articulate. So during this part of prep time, you are discussing the lines of argument and considering overall strategic placement. Let us look back to our example and give it a try.

Say you and your partner have come up with the following lines of argument to support your case thesis to abolish capital punishment in the United States:

- Capital punishment is not a deterrent to crime.
- The system is racist.
- Innocent people have been put to death.
- The process is more expensive than life in prison.
- It violates the Universal Declaration of Human Rights.
- It violates the moral standards of many citizens.
- It eliminates the possibility of doing psychological research on criminals.

Which arguments are strongest? Which should be eliminated? In what order should the arguments be presented? What supporting material do you know of to bolster these positions? (By supporting material, we are referring to the evidence and reasoning you will use to support your claims. See the chapters on argumentation and building arguments for more information.)

After considering such questions, leave yourself a minute or two for the fifth and final step: recapping your overall plan, preparing an introductory narrative, and tying up any loose ends.

To summarize, a Government team's fifteen-minute preparation time might look like the following:

1. Approximately two minutes analyzing the resolution, asking what it requires and does not require you prove
2. Approximately two minutes developing and crafting the case statement or thesis and defining terms
3. Approximately nine minutes inventing arguments, organizing the case, and developing supporting material
4. Approximately two minutes confirming the plan, crafting an introductory narrative, and tying up any loose ends

OPPOSITION PREP TIME

What should be done during the fifteen-minute prep time when you and your partner represent the Opposition? It might be easiest to begin our discussion with two examples of what you should *not* do as an Opposition team during prep time.

You should *not* spend the entire time trying to guess what case the Government team will run. It is indeed useful to contemplate some of the possible directions the resolution might lead the Government, but avoid the folly of trying to read minds. But you should also not simply throw up your hands and convince yourself you cannot do anything to prepare because the Government controls the interpretation of the resolution. Regardless of the specific resolutional interpretation of the Government team, the resolution contains a great deal of useful information that Opposition teams should discuss during prep. We will also discuss prepping for the most abstract resolutions as well.

Now that we have mentioned what to avoid, let us focus on how to use the fifteen-minute prep time efficiently when you are on the Opposition. We will continue to use the example that we began the chapter with: *This House would exterminate capital punishment.* The first two minutes of prep time on the Opposition will mirror the basic approach you use when you are the Government team. Resolutional analysis should be done by the Opposition as well. Answer the questions as to what the resolution does and does not require that you prove; the primary difference being that you are looking at it from the Opposition perspective. That leads to the other significant distinctions you should consider when you are on the other side of the aisle.

As we have mentioned throughout the book, Government teams have quite a bit of latitude in their specific interpretations of the resolution and the types of cases they choose to run. Even our seemingly straightforward sample resolution could be turned into a debate on the merits of animal testing. Consequently, when you are the Opposition team, your focus should be as much on the form the resolution takes as much as its content. Following is an explanation of this important distinction between Government and Opposition teams.

Since you cannot anticipate whether the Government will define capital punishment conventionally or with a significant twist, during prep time you and your partner should examine the form of the resolution *This House would exterminate capital punishment*. The language of the resolution indicates that however capital punishment is finally defined, the Government must support exterminating it. This is significant. Should a Government team propose an alteration of capital punishment, such as seeking uniformity in all fifty states, it could be argued by the Opposition that this fails to meet the burden of proof. Suffice it to say that Opposition teams should spend two to three minutes looking at the form and direction of the resolution as was discussed in Chapter Eight on defining the resolution.

Now that you have engaged in resolutional analysis, including an examination of the structure and form of the motion, the next step during prep time is to stake out the Opposition's debate and philosophy. If the form of the resolution indicates that the Government must support the extermination or abolition of something, you and your partner should brainstorm an opposing philosophical stance. What are the practical and philosophical concerns with eliminating a practice? This part of prep time should be spent brainstorming arguments that counter the direction the resolution takes. This phase might take three to four minutes.

Once you have discovered arguments that counter the direction of the resolution, you should use your next few minutes of prep time to develop arguments that support a contrary approach. In other words, what are some affirmative or positive reasons for either keeping the current system or employing a less radical approach? As we have noted previously, it is as important to have positive reasons for something as it is to have negative reasons to avoid a particular action.

After a few minutes contemplating the aforementioned areas, the next step is to consider an Opposition interpretation of the resolution and a possible case outline. In the event that the Government puts forth an undebatable or clearly unacceptable interpretation of the resolution, it is important to have an alternative. We advocate flexibility on the part of the Opposition. Some Government teams may insist on debates that necessitate reformulation. Should this unfortunate situation arise, you and your partner should be prepared to present an alternative to the Government case.

To recap, an Opposition's fifteen-minute preparation time period might look something like this:

1. Resolutional analysis focusing on burdens: two minutes
2. Analysis of form and structure of resolution: three minutes
3. Opposition philosophy: three minutes
4. Arguments supporting philosophy: three minutes
5. Opposition case: three minutes
6. Tying up lose ends: one minute

CONCLUSION

These are basic strategies for developing a case for both Opposition and Government during preparation time. Remember that each team will develop its own system and style. However, these are the basic elements that must be covered.

Chapter Fourteen

Speakers' Roles

Key Concepts

Leader of the Opposition—the first and last speaker for the
Opposition team

Member of Government—the second speaker for the
Government team

Member of the Opposition—the second speaker for the
Opposition team

Prime Minister—the first and last speaker for the
Government team

Following the framework of the legislature, Parliamentary debate consists of
two sides competing to persuade the members of the House of the superiority
of their respective position on the resolution being debated. The team supporting the resolution is the Government, and the team standing against the motion
is the Opposition side of the House. We would like to remind debaters, especially those coming from a background in other debate formats, which typically
follow a judicial model, that the historical model of the House of Parliament
means that audience expectations for the manner in which the advocates put
forth their respective positions are distinct from formats of debate with an
Affirmative and a Negative team. The distinction is more than simply pure se-

mantics, for the nature of parliamentary debate requires the speakers to play the role of advocate in a given context.

Members of Parliament find themselves on both sides of the aisle during their careers and, more important, joining up with members who may have argued against them in the previous voting debate. Therefore, it is imperative that debaters remain cordial and respectful of their opponents in each debate.

The Government team consists of the **Prime Minister** and a **Member of Government**, while the Opposition team consists of the **Leader of the Opposition** and the **Member of the Opposition**. Although each team will ultimately choose its own strategic approach, the adjudicator's expectations remain framed by conventional approaches to either side of the motion. Moreover, clarity and fairness may be enhanced by following the routinized structures of each speaker role.

SPEAKERS' ROLES

The Prime Minister is the first and last speaker in the debate. At the writing of this text, the first constructive speech by the Prime Minister is seven minutes in length. It is the province of the Prime Minister constructive to define the motion and present the case for the Government within the seven-minute time frame. Of course, as is the case with all four constructive speeches, the first and last minutes of the speech are protected. This means that Opposition questions (points of information) are prohibited during the first and last minute of the constructive speeches. The significance of this speech is self-evident. Debates are often won or lost in this seven-minute opening speech.

Following the Prime Minister constructive, the Leader of the Opposition has an eight-minute constructive speech. During this time, the Leader of the Opposition either accepts or rejects the Prime Minister's definition of the motion and begins the Opposition's case against the motion. Regardless of the specific strategy of the Opposition, it is imperative that the Leader of the Opposition clash with the Government. By definition, debate necessitates clash, and it is the responsibility of the Leader of the Opposition to generate disputation in this first Opposition constructive.

The Member of Government's eight-minute constructive comes after the first Leader of the Opposition speech. The Member of Government reestablishes and expands the Government's case in light of the Opposition's argu-

Speaking Times

Prime Minister constructive	7 minutes
Leader of Opposition constructive	8 minutes
Member of Government constructive	8 minutes
Member of Opposition constructive	8 minutes
Leader of Opposition rebuttal	4 minutes
Prime Minister rebuttal	5 minutes

ments. The superior Member of Government speeches will not only counter Leader of the Opposition arguments and reiterate Prime Minister positions but also introduce independent lines of argumentation further bolstering the Government case.

The final constructive speech of the debate is reserved for the Member of the Opposition. At the very least, the Member of the Opposition continues constructing the Opposition's case against the motion, in addition to refuting any new lines of argumentation put forth in the Member of Government's speech. Since no new issues may be brought up in the rebuttal speeches, both the Member of the Opposition and the Member of Government need to be certain at the very least to mention claims that the Prime Minister and Leader of the Opposition wish to highlight during their final speeches. (Should the Member of the Opposition enter new issues into the debate in the final constructive, adjudicators will permit the Prime Minister to address those issues in the rebuttal. Since the Opposition rebuttal directly follows the Member of the Opposition constructive, the Prime Minister rebuttal is the first and only opportunity for the Government to respond to these new arguments.)

As previously mentioned, the final speeches consist of two rebuttals of four and five minutes, respectively. In essence, rebuttal speeches give each team a final opportunity to analyze the totality of the debate, put forth its perception of the most significant issues of the debate, and explain why its side of the House should prevail.

The Opposition team gets two consecutive speeches in what is popularly known as the "twelve-minute block" as the Leader of the Opposition follows up the Member of the Opposition's eight-minute constructive with a four-minute rebuttal. The Leader of the Opposition seeks to highlight the significant issues in the debate and advocate how and why the Opposition prevailed on these major issues, thus constituting an Opposition ballot.

The Prime Minister has the arduous task of following the twelve-minute Opposition block with the final speech of the debate, the five-minute Prime Minister rebuttal. Analysis and focus become especially important here. The Prime Minister indiscriminently responding to *every* Opposition argument and spewing counterarguments at five hundred words per minute will befuddle rather than persuade. In contrast, Prime Ministers carefully choosing the two, three, or four most significant issues in the debate and articulating the Government's superiority regarding those same areas of controversy will increase their chances of winning the debate. Very impressive is the Prime Minister who is able to boil the debate down to the core issues and illustrate how the Government's superior argumentation warrants support for the motion.

MORE THAN A COLLECTION OF ARGUMENTS

Before discussing some basic strategic considerations for the various speeches in the debate, we would like to remind debaters not to forget what they learned in their first public speaking courses. Quite often, debaters become so wrapped up in analyzing, constructing, and refuting arguments that they overlook the totality of the presentation and the fact that each block of time necessitates a unified speech.

Successful debaters view each opportunity at the podium as more than individual brushstrokes completing a tiny section of the canvas. The top debaters always keep one eye on the entire painting. These same debaters approach both constructives and rebuttals as speeches containing an introduction, a body, and a conclusion.

A rapid-fire point-by-point technical approach to debate can be very annoying. When all else fails, remember the mantra of every high school speech teacher: "Tell your audience what you're going to tell them, then tell them, and then tell them what you've told them." It's basic but too often forgotten in collegiate debate. Let us look at how the fundamental unified argumentation approach may be applied to speaker roles in parliamentary debate.

PRIME MINISTER

The Prime Minister traditionally begins the constructive by recognizing the Speaker of the House, the members of the Opposition, Members of Parliament in the audience (who are theoretically voting but not debating), and the Prime Minister's own partner: "Madame (or Mister—an important distinction to acknowledge accurately!) Speaker, worthy members of the Opposition, my esteemed partner, and members of Parliament."

Of course, several initial greetings exist, but what is most important is acknowledging *all* members of the theoretical House. Remember, these initial greetings represent the beginning of your speech. Your audience is making judgments about your credibility during this introduction. Do not underestimate the significance of first impressions. Prime Ministers who sloppily or sarcastically race through these initial welcomes suffer an immediate loss of credibility with the audience. Why begin a speech by damaging your own credibility?

The heart of the introduction usually follows the initial acknowledgment of the House. Unfortunately, far too often Prime Ministers follow the initial greetings by launching immediately into the definitions of terms.

"Madame Speaker, the worthy Opposition, my loyal colleague, and members of Parliament. In order to clarify this debate, we offer up the following definitions." Though this is not a major tragedy for the Government, several superior introductions exist. Prime Ministers employing an attention-getter, thesis, or case statement and a preview of the major points of the speech usually produce a far more compelling and elegant introduction of case. The following example is for the resolution *This House believes that censorship is more dangerous than pornography.*

> "Madame Speaker, when former Supreme Court Justice Potter Stewart uttered those infamous words about the subject of pornography, 'I can't define it, but I know it when I see it,' he was unknowingly articulating the central argument against the institution of laws seeking to censor so-called pornographic material. Laws necessitate definitions, and U.S. history has illustrated the inability of both the legislative and judicial branches to agree on an acceptable legal definition of pornography that doesn't violate the First Amendment to the Constitution.

We on this side of the aisle will illustrate why indeed censorship is more dangerous than pornography. We will do this with three primary areas of analysis. First, we will illustrate the unconstitutionality of restrictions on so-called pornography. Second, we will explore the damaging impact of censorship on our democracy. And finally, the Government in this debate exhibits how the free marketplace of ideas provides the superior context in which to examine controversial issues such as so-called pornography."

This Prime Minister has clearly set forth the Government interpretation of the motion along with a preview of the major positions. She may continue by defining terms either contextually (explaining how they are used in the case) or in a standard dictionary-type definition. As Prime Minister, and really in every other speaker role, it is important to remember the power of a rhetorically elegant speech as compared to a loose collection of clipped phrases and words.

Most adjudicators enter the debating chambers with anticipation and hope for a compelling intellectual exchange of ideas. The Prime Minister constructive quite often determines whether that adjudicator will be disappointed or grateful. Prime Ministers who frame the controversy artfully, providing for substantive areas of clash, will be duly rewarded by most judges.

Debaters may wish to view the Prime Minister constructive as analogous to the period of setting up the rules for Monopoly or any other game. Though basic guidelines exist, players have their own local quirks. Some choose to award $500 for landing on "Free Parking," while others like to suggest a ban on property buying on the first trip around the board. In parliamentary debate, it is the Prime Minister, representing the Government, who first suggests the parameters for the debate about to take place. Prime Ministers should take full advantage of this responsibility.

Following the Prime Minister's first constructive is the Leader of the Opposition's constructive speech.

LEADER OF THE OPPOSITION

The Leader of Opposition constructive also begins with the greetings to all parties present. The objective of the Leader of Opposition constructive is twofold: to present an Opposition philosophy and to poke holes in the Government case. The Leader of Opposition constructive begins by setting forth the Opposition philosophy. This philosophy gives the adjudicator an idea of how the Opposition will approach the Government's case. For example, following the Prime Minister's opening on censorship, the Leader of the Opposition might counter with something like this:

> "The Opposition is clearly in favor of the right and privilege of free speech. However, we would also remind the House of Justice Holmes's admonition that 'the most stringent protection to free speech would not protect a man in falsely shouting fire in a theater, and causing a panic.' Clearly Justice Holmes was admitting that a free speech must be limited to prevent harms to its citizens. The Opposition will argue today that unchecked free speech is a danger and that some limits on free speech are the only way to protect the citizenry. We believe that the current test established by the Supreme Court in *Miller* v. *California* is a fair way to protect both citizens subjected to and peddlers of pornography. We will prove this by first refuting the Government's claims and then asserting independent reasons why censorship is sometimes necessary in the realm of pornography."

The Leader of Opposition constructive will then refute the claims of the Government by attacking the claims, evidence, and reasoning. The Leader of the Opposition will then build a case that offers arguments to support the Opposition's position on the case. Note that the Opposition does not always build an independent case. Indeed, in some instances, merely refuting the Government's arguments will be enough to win the debate.

MEMBER CONSTRUCTIVES

Each of the constructives delivered by the second speakers of the opposing teams has the same basic goals: refutation and rebuttal. The Member of Government and the Member of the Opposition attempt to rebuild their partner's positions while continuing to poke holes in their opponents' cases (see Chapter Eleven on refutation and rebuttal). Perhaps the most important strategy for the Member of Government and Member of the Opposition is to extend their partner's cases. Quite often second speakers are tempted merely to reiterate the case presented by their partners. However, a successful second speaker will bring *new* insights and information into the debate. For example, say the

111

Prime Minister has argued that censorship would limit access to pornographic materials such as *Hustler* magazine. The Leader of the Opposition might then argue that current standards only restrict who can access this pornographic material and that the material itself warranted such restrictions. The Member of the Opposition could then argue that certain communities have deemed literature such as the novel *The Color Purple* pornographic. The Member of the Opposition has extended the argument to include not only materials traditionally deemed pornographic but also materials that communities have singled out as pornographic. Both types of materials still support the argument that censorship limits access to pornographic materials but broadens what the Government means by *pornographic*.

Extending arguments allows for the Member of Government and the Member of the Opposition to provide new insights into the debate and to make their positions critical in the debate. If the opposing team has destroyed the first speaker's case, the Member's speech can be crucial for salvaging a case.

CONCLUSION

Each speech in a parliamentary debate is important to sway the judge's opinion about the outcome of the debate. Though each speaker and speech must conform to the circumstances of the debate, these general guidelines should provide speakers with an understanding of what each speech should attempt to accomplish.

Chapter Fifteen

Note Taking (Flowing) and Effective Listening

Key Concepts

Critical listening—listening to evaluate and judge
Flowing—note taking during a debate
Listening for understanding—listening to comprehend
Psychological noise—distractions from within the person that inhibit effective listening

---

Most communication scholars agree that people recall about 50 percent of what they have heard. At least *half* of the message is lost! Time after time, researchers have concluded that human beings are not particularly efficient listeners. What does this mean for parliamentary debaters?

Listening well and taking effective notes often mean the difference between winning and losing a debate. As adjudicators, we have witnessed several debates where the inability to take good notes or poor listening behavior was the deciding factor in determining which team won the debate.

Fortunately, debaters can do a great deal to improve their listening efficiency as well as their note-taking skills. This chapter will discuss both listening effectively and constructive note taking in a parliamentary debate.

LISTENING

A great many textbooks in communication make a distinction between listening for understanding and listening critically. **Listening for understanding** is usually defined as listening with the primary goal being comprehension. An example of this type of listening is when you are listening to your doctor discuss what type of regimen you should be on to improve your health. Another example of listening for understanding would be when you are in a biology or a chemistry class lecture. In these examples, your primary goal in listening is to receive and comprehend the material presented as accurately as possible.

In contrast to this, the primary goal of **critical listening** is listening that "challenges the speaker's message and evaluates its accuracy, meaningfulness, and utility" (Pearson and Nelson 92). An example of this type of listening would be if you are listening to a salesperson's pitch or a political candidate. In both cases your primary goal in listening is that of evaluation and judgment. You are asking yourself if you can indeed accept the message.

Which listening approach would be more useful in a parliamentary debate? Critical listening may seem like the obvious response. But in fact, the best parliamentary debaters employ *both* listening techniques in debates and work judiciously to improve in both areas.

Listening is an intentional, active process that requires a physiological and psychological effort. You can *hear* merely by being present, but *listening* requires a conscious effort. Only when you attach meaning to aural stimuli are you truly listening.

Listening is a skill that is learned, much like skiing, driving a car, handwriting, or any other activity that requires conscious effort and practice. The good news is that you can continually improve your ability to listen. However, the bad news is that you may have to overcome some bad habits that you may have picked up along the way.

What are some of the common obstacles to effective listening and how can you overcome them? If you have partied until 4:00 a.m. on Tuesday night and drag yourself to your 9:00 a.m. history course on Wednesday, you may have noticed that it is difficult to listen and take meaningful notes. Your physiological state will influence your ability to listen. If you are tired, you will have difficulty putting forth the necessary effort to listen attentively. This situation is exaggerated in debates, which require that you listen to a number of rapid arguments at an accelerated pace. You must be physically prepared to listen well. Get enough sleep. Eat properly. Take care of yourself and avoid entering the debate chambers at a disadvantage because you are physically unprepared to put forth the effort required to listen attentively for an extended period of time.

Another obstacle to efficient listening concerns what communication researchers refer to as **psychological noise**. Just as the physical noise of an airplane passing overhead might prevent you from hearing what someone has said, if you are thinking about what happened in the last debate while ostensibly listening to the Prime Minister constructive in the current debate, chances are you will misperceive the message. Mental distractions can subvert comprehension. You must be not only physically prepared to listen but psychologically prepared as well. Concentrate on the moment at hand. Remember the Zen philosophy of being in the moment. You cannot change what happened in the last debate. Be prepared mentally and physically to listen in the current debate in which you are competing. It is the only one you can influence with your effort.

Still one more barrier to listening effectively might be termed "overemotional listening." Perhaps you dislike the Prime Minister. You think he is a jerk. You have noticed several annoying traits that he possesses, and you find yourself attending to them more than to his arguments. How effective do you think you will be in this debate? Be aware of those subjective associations, and do your best to focus on the message rather then the messenger. Remember, your best revenge would be doing well in the debate!

Apart from preparing yourself physically and psychologically to listen, it is also necessary to be conscious of your listening goals. Keep a particular focus in mind. Much of what is said in any given debate speech is extraneous information. It is your responsibility to separate the wheat from the chaff. Which information presented is significant? Which is absolutely vital for you to know?

An efficient listener listens for the major ideas and facts within each speech. What are the central claims? What are the important definitional words and phrases? What are the warrants and support for the arguments presented?

When you enter the debating chambers following preparation time, you should have an idea of what you are listening for. Is there a key phrase in the resolution that must be defined completely? Did the speaker preview one particular argument that demands clarification? Mentally prepare yourself to focus on the message.

To increase your ability to listen for important ideas and facts, it is best to plan a system with your partner beforehand. Because you and your partner have different speaking positions, it is wise to plan out how you will maximize your listening through teamwork. For example, if you are the Prime Minister, it will be especially helpful if your partner pays extra attention to the Leader of the Opposition's rebuttal speech since you will be busy preparing your own rebuttal speech. Should the Leader of the Opposition attempt to sneak a new argument into the rebuttal speech, the Member of Government should be prepared to point that out. There is no one perfect system for listening as a team; however, it remains highly advantageous to possess a strategy for listening with your partner to avoid missed opportunities.

FLOWING

Now that you have prepared yourself to listen and have devised a strategy with your partner, it is time to prepare yourself to flow the debate. **Flowing** refers to the practice of taking organized notes during the debate. Although not very complicated, learning to flow a debate in an accurate and orderly fashion takes time. However, once you master the art of flowing, your recall and organization will improve substantially. Following are some suggestions:

- Use a large legal or sketch pad. Having a decent amount of surface area to write on helps avoid having to write in tiny illegible script at the bottom of a page. A larger surface area also permits your eyes to scan your notes more easily while you are speaking. Leaning over and squinting to read your notes will do nothing to help your speaking delivery!
- Use columns to keep track of the speeches. Many experienced debaters will actually make large vertical columns to separate the different speeches of the debate. This helps you keep track of exactly who said what—valuable information in a parliamentary debate.
- Use pens of different color. (We like to call this "Technicolor writing.") Remember, the more you can do to help yourself stay well organized by tracking the evolution of the debate, the better. Apart from vertical columns, using different colored pens for the distinct speeches can further illuminate the progress of the debate. Some debaters use one color for the Government team and one for the Opposition; others go so far as to use a distinct color for each speaking position. Experiment and find what works best for you.

- Employ abbreviations. Your goals should be brevity and clarity. Abbreviations can assist you by reducing the amount you have to write down. We have provided a chart of some helpful symbols you might use. In addition, we strongly recommend that you take a good look at the resolution and find abbreviations for words and phrases you anticipate will be employed throughout the debate. For example, if the resolution is *This House believes that cloning is more of a marketing problem than a moral problem*, it would prove helpful to figure out an abbreviation for *cloning* (Cl) and perhaps the terms *marketing* (mrk) and *moral* (mrl). By using abbreviations throughout the debate, you will save yourself valuable time and effort. However, be sure you can understand those abbreviations. Avoid meaningless garble that hinders more than it helps.

Leave plenty of room on your flow pad for the Prime Minister constructive. The first speech of the debate is important for several reasons, one of which is that it usually sets up the initial organizational framework for the entire debate. It is important to leave enough room between the major claims and supporting arguments because you cannot always accurately anticipate which arguments will elicit the greatest amount of attention and substance. Leaving yourself plenty of space between the major claims of the Prime Minister constructive prevents unpleasant surprises. Some debaters use separate pages for each of the major contentions presented. Again, experiment in practice debates with different systems until you find one that suits your needs.

A common mistake that many novices make is writing down too much at the expense of listening carefully. It is just as important to know what to flow as it

A Sampling of Symbols

$	money, funding	UN	United Nations
<	less than	w/	with
>	greater than	w/o	without
=	is, equal	ben	benefits
%	percentage	b/c	because

is to know how to flow. Following are some suggestions as to what debaters should flow in debates:

- Flow the definitions, criteria, and plan (if there is one). As the debate evolves, the initial definitions and framing of the resolution sometimes become neglected. Making the effort to flow these fundamentals accurately provides you with an opportunity to scrutinize the consistency of positions presented.

- Flow the structure of each argument. Flowing the claim, evidence presented, and the warrant or reasoning employed by the speaker provides you with sufficient information to analyze the crux of your opponent's case. It also increases the chances that you will note inconsistencies or errors in reasoning at the different levels of argument.

- Be certain that you flow your partner's speeches as well as those of your opponents. Since your goal is to observe the progression of the entire debate, it is critical that you monitor your partner's speeches accurately as well. Moreover, this will help you to avoid contradicting your partner. Nothing is more damaging to a team than contradictory arguments. Flowing your partner's speech should help prevent this occurrence.

- Finally, we strongly recommend flowing the points of information in the debate. Many judges will ignore, or simply forget, potentially effective points of information unless they are later referred to during a constructive speech. Judges are impressed by debaters who not only refer to a point of information but then proceed to explain the impact it makes on a particular argument or contention. For example, "Madame Speaker, my partner asked the Prime Minister in a point of information if he was familiar with the Supreme Court's ruling in the case *Buckley* v. *Valeo,* and he responded that he wasn't. Well, as I'm sure you're well aware, the Court ruled among other things that spending money, even millions of dollars, on one's own campaign represents political expression, which is protected under the First Amendment. Therefore, Madame Speaker, the Government's plan is unconstitutional."

AFTER THE DEBATE

In this chapter, we have discussed the importance of effective listening and note taking (flowing) and given suggestions on how to flow. Now we would like to offer some suggestions for using the flow *after* the debate.

Think of your flow sheets as a valuable historical record that can be examined days and weeks after the debate. We suggest keeping a file of your old flow sheets, labeled with the school and the particular team you encountered. Even though the resolutions change from debate to debate, you may notice patterns emerging among some teams. In addition, it provides your teammates with access to information that might prove helpful to them should they face the same opponents in the future.

Perhaps even more valuable is the insight your flow sheets can provide regarding your own efforts. What were the beneficial and harmful aspects of the case you constructed? Which arguments were well developed and which ones were not? Although hindsight cannot change the outcome of the debate, it can help you in the future. Of course, the historical record is only as useful as you make it. If you simply view the notes as evidence for why the judge made the wrong decision, you will probably do more damage than accrue any benefit. Only attempts at a more detached view of past debates will prove to be beneficial.

CONCLUSION

Flowing is a critical part of your ability to do well in parliamentary debate; it helps you to follow the evolution of arguments, as well as the organization of the debate. Flowing can be successful only if you develop both critical and comprehensive listening skills.

Chapter Sixteen

Delivery

Key Concepts

Language use—effective word choice
Nonverbal communication—the use of nonlinguistic
    messages to create meaning
Oral delivery—use of the voice to emphasize and impart
    meaning to words
Organization—the distribution and ordering of arguments
Physical delivery—use of the body to impart messages
Vocal variety—changes in rate, pitch, and volume to give
    meaning to words

There is an absolute *interdependence* between style and substance for the successful communicator. If you have ever seen the footage of Martin Luther King Jr.'s "I Have a Dream" speech in its entirety, you are well aware of the profound impact style and delivery have on a speaker's message. Though some commentators bemoan the fact that human beings make judgments about claims based upon factors other than pure Cartesian logic, the fact remains that subjective elements, including the attractiveness of an orator's delivery, do influence the decision-making process. The "brilliant case" that you and your partner have constructed outside the debating chambers will be squandered should you fail to communicate your analysis clearly to the critic. As Aristotle duly noted, language and delivery have an enormous influence on your credibility as a speaker, as well as on the overall emotional impact of your communication.

This chapter will explore some of the primary aesthetic elements that create what is commonly referred to as a speaker's style or delivery. We have grouped these elements into three major categories: organization, nonverbal communication, and language.

ORGANIZATION

Organization—the distribution and ordering of arguments—remains central to the effectiveness of all types of rhetorical communication, including speeches in parliamentary debate. As you are preparing to speak, you need to consider several questions concerning organization: Where should I place my arguments? Which one should go first? How much time should I allot for each position? Which arguments shall I group together? How can I arrange my speech to promote a logical progression of ideas?

While the specific organizational strategy is necessarily unique to each individual speech, research in communication and persuasion can guide you when making those decisions. For example, because listeners tend to be more attentive at the beginning of a speech, you might consider presenting a particularly strong argument toward the beginning. Getting the judge on your side immediately will enhance the receptivity of the Speaker of the House to your remaining arguments.

Similarly, you should conclude your speeches with a strong argument containing an emotional impact. Leaving a powerful impression at the conclusion of your speech is just as significant as making a positive initial impression. Far too often parliamentary debaters find themselves running out of time while barely touching on a major issue. At the conclusion of the debate, when all of the debaters have left the room and the critic is alone with the ballot, certain elements of the debate will stand out and influence the final decision. A disciplined debater will begin presentation of a final argument with enough time to develop the position to have maximum impact on the debate.

Should you recognize that your opponent has ignored an argument or a key issue, be certain to point this out to your audience. This will enhance your credibility by illustrating your alertness, skill in listening, and analysis of the debating situation.

In addition, be certain to respond to arguments you perceive as having been particularly effective for your opponents. Like that rattling you hear in your car's engine, ignoring it will not cause it to go away. (Both authors have tested this hypothesis several times). Attack the strong arguments of your opponents immediately lest you give the impression that you are incapable of doing so.

At the most basic level, choices about organization communicate prioritization, and critics will make judgments about your debating quality on the basis of this prioritization. Consequently, not only does the order in which you present your arguments matter, but the amount of time you spend on developing your arguments does as well.

Decisions concerning approximately how much time you plan to spend on particular lines of argumentation need to be done *before* you actually begin speaking. Parliamentary debaters need to avoid the "shotgun approach" to communicating argument. Simply spewing arguments and counterarguments at a rapid pace without any sense of forethought, cohesiveness, or prioritization will result in low speaker points and little persuasiveness. Far more persuasive and rhetorically effective is the debater who takes the "archery approach." Survey the entire situation, and pick and choose your targets carefully. After you have prioritized your arguments, be sure to spend an amount of time on each issue commensurate with your perception of its significance in terms of the entire debate. If you believe that your argument concerning the environmental benefits of your position are central to the debate, take the time to develop this line of argumentation.

NONVERBAL COMMUNICATION

Another critical element influencing your rhetorical effectiveness is your nonverbal communication. **Nonverbal communication** includes all of the nonlinguistic means of expressing a message—everything from your posture, the clothing you wear, your eye contact, and other visually oriented modes of communication to the tone of your voice, the rate at which you speak, and other vocal yet nonlinguistic means of communication.

As critics, we are consistently surprised by students who seem to disregard everything they know about public communication when engaged in a debate. Never lose sight of the fact that nonverbal communication has a great impact on the ability to persuade. Since your primary goal as a parliamentary debater is to persuade audiences to accept your claims, it follows logically that you should devote some attention to your own nonverbal communication. We will discuss some of the areas of nonverbal communication particularly important for parliamentary debaters.

ORAL DELIVERY

"This is CNN."
"And that's the rest of the story."
"I *am* somebody."

Most likely you can hear the voices of James Earl Jones, Paul Harvey, and Jesse Jackson when reading these quotations. Each of these communicators understands very clearly the power of the human voice. Vocal variety and emphasis can make an otherwise mediocre constructive speech into a compelling case for Government. **Vocal variety** refers to changes in rate, pitch, and volume. Your voice is a tool; use it! Highlight nonverbally points that you believe to be particularly important to your case. Use contrast in your voice. Avoid a monotone delivery, which suggests that every word you utter is of equal importance.

The quality of your voice is important because it shows excellence in vocal training. Your voice should be free of tension and grating qualities such as harshness, stridency, and vocal fry. If you know what vocal problems you have, you should begin work immediately to eliminate them. If you think you have no major problems, you have two choices. First, you can go to a tournament and see if any judges comment on your voice. Or you can go to a voice teacher at your school and ask for an evaluation of your speaking voice. This is usually a painless process of reading a passage and talking. Either way, you will have obtained at least a preliminary evaluation.

Another aspect of your verbal delivery to be considered is your rate of speech. Most speakers tend to speak too quickly, especially when they are nervous. You should remember that your audience is hearing most of this information for the first time. You must give your audience time to absorb what you are saying. At times a slow pace may seem sluggish, but chances are it is just right. If you have a naturally slow and strident vocal delivery, you may have to inject it with some enthusiasm. The best way to determine if you are at the right pace is to record yourself on videotape or audiotape.

Do not underestimate the impact of . . . . the dramatic pause. You might view your entire speech as analogous to a wonderful five-course meal. Allow the audience time to digest your ideas. If your listeners are still contemplating your first central argument when you have already moved on to your third, not only has the second argument or example been lost, but the impact of the first and probably the third have been reduced.

PHYSICAL DELIVERY

Physically, you have a lot to remember. First and foremost, relax—tension shows physically the most. When you are nervous, your hands and feet will do all sorts of annoying things. Let us start with your hands.

Hands have a natural tendency to float to one particular position that is comfortable for you, whether it be clasped in front of you or in back, resting on your hips or folded. You should discover whatever position is best for you. This will be your base position. When you are speaking, you should use your hands to aid in the explanation of what you are saying. You do not need to move on every word. However, if movement is not frequent enough to seem natural, it will seem planned. On the opposite side of the coin is too much movement. You will distract your listeners if your hands are constantly moving. You will tire them out as they try to keep up with you. Most movements are fine as long as you keep them relatively big. Small movements, as in just moving your hands, are distracting and will give the impression that you are timid and not really moving. Also, try to keep your elbows away from your sides.

The most important thing to remember when it comes to movement is that it should appear natural and spontaneous. As such, any and all movement should be purposeful. You should practice enough so that you are not consciously thinking that you have to move. However, you should not have every move so rehearsed that it looks premeditated (or "canned" in parliamentary debate parlance).

The second most active area of the body during public speaking is usually the feet. You will probably elect to stay behind the podium, but some debaters prefer to walk in front of the podium to eliminate the barrier between the speaker and the audience. Whichever is more comfortable for you, remember to keep your feet planted. Pacing or frantic movement detracts from the content of your speech. It is easy to get caught up in the momentum of the argument and find yourself pacing. However, for the audience, pacing can be quite distracting.

OTHER PHYSICAL CONSIDERATIONS

Other significant elements of nonverbal communication are your general attitude and eye contact. As we continually remind our team members, from the moment you walk into the debating chambers, you are being judged. Picture a slovenly dressed debater who walks into the room prior to the reading of the motion, loudly complaining about the critic in the last debate. He ignores the critic who is sitting in the second row observing his behavior, throws his backpack down, and slouches in his chair with his feet on the table. What type of credibility will this speaker have with his audience? It is just as easy to create a positive impression with your nonverbal communication. Audiences react more positively to speakers with erect posture and professional dress.

Apart from your clothing and your posture, eye contact is extremely influential in creating impressions. Our culture even refers to "shifty-eyed" people as untrustworthy and parents insist that their children "look them in the eye" when talking to them in hopes of discovering the truth. In like manner, audiences will most likely believe a debater who looks them in the eye when speaking as opposed to one who stares at a notepad or gazes out the window. Be mindful of this powerful element of nonverbal communication.

You should schedule practice sessions with a coach, teammates, and a videotape machine, if possible. Videotapes are a great help because they let you identify bad speaking habits that you might have. You will become more conscious of them if you see yourself doing them and will have an easier time eliminating these habits from your speaking style.

LANGUAGE USE

So far we have discussed the organizational structure of speeches and the nonverbal elements of rhetorical communication. The final element of communicating argument we will explore concerns the **language use**.

If you are skeptical about the impact language has on our perception and the construction of meaning, we suggest you consider why car dealerships refer to "preowned vehicles" rather than "used cars." Think about why the U.S. Department of Defense no longer goes by its original name, the War Department. Or reflect on the corporate term *downsizing*, so much preferred to "firing employees." This euphemistic language is employed intentionally. Clever communicators understand the powerful impact language choices have on our perception of reality. As a debater, your language choices affect not only your credibility with the audience but also the very acceptability of your ideas and claims.

Part of choosing your words carefully consists of knowing what to avoid. Avoid jargon, clichés, and filler language. *Jargon* refers to language that is commonly used within a particular group or profession but obscure to outsiders. Parliamentary debate is a form of public argument. Some of your critics might be hired judges from outside the academy. If you employ jargon, you risk alienating a critic or creating a misunderstanding of your position. Be certain your language is comprehensible to your critic. Strive for clarity, not showmanship. *Clichés* are overused phrases that often muddle ideas and prevent clarity. Rather than resorting to some hackneyed phrase or opinion, develop your idea with language meaningful to both you and your audience. Your skill as an orator will improve if you seek out fresh ways to articulate your thoughts. Be specific and concrete.

Finally, avoid purposeless filler language and vocalized pauses. Speaking time is limited in debate, so a wise use of that time is critical. *Filler language* ("Well, it's like, you know") serves no particular purpose but may detract from your message. Such wasteful words and phrases will not advance your argument. All of us have picked up conversational habits that hamper our ability to articulate our thoughts concisely. As much as possible, strive to eliminate vocalized pauses ("um," "ah") from your communication. You might be surprised, reviewing a video or audiotape of a practice constructive speech, by how much of your speech does little to advance your case. Awareness is the first step, followed by a conscious effort at eliminating bad habits.

Now that we have discussed what to avoid, a few words are warranted on goals to strive for when communicating argument. First, be concise. This does *not* mean you should fail to develop your lines of argumentation. It refers to the language choices you make when doing so. Instead of saying, "One major reason that we have found to be a cause of why people in the United States don't vote very much is . . . ," say "U.S. citizens are apathetic because. . . ." Be concise and direct.

CONCLUSION

Delivery is a critical element in the conduct of parliamentary debate. Too often debaters think that the arguments are all that count. But in close debates, these elements of delivery will make a decisive impression in the mind of the judge. Remember that parliamentary debate is public debate. Consequently, winning the hearts and minds of your listeners requires that you keep their attention, and polished, appropriate delivery goes a long way toward keeping their attention and leaving a lasting good impression.

Chapter Seventeen

Points of Information and Points of Order

Key Concepts

Heckling—comments made to the opposing team without benefit of a point of information

Point of information—a question or statement addressed to the opposing team that attempts to seek or offer information

Point of order—a question of procedure addressed to the judge

Point of personal privilege—a question addressed to the judge, seeking a change in the conditions of the debate

In parliamentary debate, the opposing side may ask questions anytime after the first minute and before the last minute of the constructive speeches. This allows audience, speaker, and the questioner to retain the context in which the question was asked. Parliamentary debate also adds another element: the point of order. Points of order are directed to the judge rather than to the other team. The judge must rule on the point of order immediately. In this manner, all sides can ensure the fairness of the debate; we will see exactly how later in this chapter.

This chapter will discuss the purpose, form, and methods of points of information and points of order. We will also entertain a brief discussion of the rarely used point of personal privilege.

POINTS OF INFORMATION

A **point of information** can be either a question or a statement that attempts to seek information or offer information. Skillful use of points of information can advance the position of a team by pointing out inconsistencies in an opponent's case, offering counterpoints during the opposing side, and keeping the opposing team in the forefront of the judge's mind. As we discuss the purpose, form, and methods of points of information, these advantages will be made obvious. There are six purposes (at least) for points of information.

Purpose

A debater can use a point of information to ask for clarification of a point that the speaker holding the floor is trying to make. For example, if the speaking team makes its first point, the opposing team might ask the speaker to repeat the point if the opposing team did not get a chance to record it on the flow sheet. Although this is a basic purpose of the point of information, it can be useful strategically. Usually, if a point is long and involved, the judge probably did not get it all down either. So asking for a point of information can help the judge, as well as draw attention to confusion in the speaker's presentation.

Second, points of information can be used to highlight inconsistencies in a team's case. Suppose a first team member said that the party conventions are often indicative of the organization of the party in general. Then the second team member says that conventions are irrelevant to presidential elections. A point of information might ask which was true, indicative or irrelevant. Inconsistencies within one speech can also be pointed out with a point of information.

Another purpose of the point of information is as a reminder of the opposing team's case. During a constructive, the speaker holding the floor may misconstrue, misrepresent, or blatantly ignore what the opposing team has said in its constructive. Tactful use of a point of information can remind the judge of what the opposing team has really said. The speaker might say, "Point of information: Didn't we argue that . . . ?" The speaker must then repudiate what has just been said or explain why the opposing team's argument is not relevant or valid. Either way, this serves to clarify the matter under contention.

A fourth purpose of the point of order is to offer information. If the speaker asks for a response from the opposing team in the opposing team's constructive, that team could respond in a point of information. Consider the case of a debate about presidential third parties. Suppose the speaker says that the opposing team has yet to show the effectiveness of any third-party candidate. The opposing team could stand and offer a point of information by saying, "What about Anderson in 1980 and Perot in 1992?" Although it remains incumbent on the opposing team to explain the effectiveness of these candidates, the opponents have started filling in the hole being dug by the speaker.

A speaker can also use a point of information to raise a new point. This can happen to refute what the speaker is attempting to prove.

Finally, a point of information can offer a witty retort. Humor plays an essential role in parliamentary debate. Although clever asides (heckles) that are unobtrusive are encouraged in parliamentary debate, sometimes a more effective way to make the point is through a point of information because in that situation the opposing team briefly has the full attention of the audience.

Form

When moving to a point of information, the debater who wishes to make the point rises with one hand on his or her head and the other hand outstretched. This oddity of parliamentary debate is based on the original Parliament where members would stand. To keep their wigs on their heads, they would have to hold the wig in place with one hand while trying to attract attention with the other. This convention remains.

Once an opposing member has risen, the speaker must acknowledge the member but not necessarily the member's point. The speaker must simply acknowledge that the other team would like to make a point. The speaker can do this by saying things such as, "I'll get to you in a minute. Let me finish this point" or "I'll take your point." The speaker does *not* have to accept a point. The speaker can choose to refuse by saying, "Not at this time" or "I don't have time right now."

The opposing team offering the point should make that point in fifteen seconds or less. Consequently, the offering member should avoid peremptory remarks that waste time. Statements such as "I just wanted to ask you" or "If you could answer this question"not only waste time but also weaken the impact of the question. Short and to-the-point questions force the speaker holding the floor to think and respond quickly.

Once the question has been asked, the opposing team member should sit down. Remember that this is a singular point and not a dialogue. If the speaker does not answer the question to the satisfaction of the opposing team, the opponent can rise again or can point to the evasion in his or her own constructive. Argumentativeness at this point is rarely appropriate; it annoys the audience and is unfair to the speaking team because it wastes the team's speaking time.

Questions should be asked at the time when they are relevant in the speech of the speaking team. A common but generally unsuccessful strategy is to wait until the speaker is a point or two away from the point of information before asking the question, obliging the speaker to go back to a point already made. However, a good speaker will answer succinctly and get back on track. This response tactic usually serves to point out the slow thought process of the opposing team. Although it is common to not think of a point right away, refutation is better saved for the opposing team's next speech rather than raised as a misplaced point of information.

Responding to Points of Information

As deadly as points of information can be, a well-stated response can be even deadlier. Various strategies are designed to respond to the point of information. We will consider the most common and effective ones here.

In the grand final of the world debating championships one year, Jeremy Philips of the University of New South Wales responded to a question from the Right Honorable Rufus Black of Oxford University. After listening to a lengthy and seemingly poignant question, Philips curtly said, "No" and continued with his point. While Black thought he had found a major hole in the Opposition's case, Philips quickly filled the hole. This strategy, though entertaining and effective at that level of debate, would probably not work for the average American-style debater. But we can learn some lessons from Philips's strategy: answer succinctly and get back on track. One of the major problems novices have in responding to points of information is getting caught up in the answer. Too often speakers will spend far too much time answering a question, thereby losing valuable time in developing their own points, and allowing the opposing team to control the speaker's agenda. Skilled speakers should be able to incorporate the answer to a question in their own points.

When responding to a question, a speaker should listen for the meat of the question and identify the purpose. The purpose will give a clue as to how the speaker should respond. If the opposing team is seeking clarification, merely restate in simpler words the point being made. If the opposing team is attempting to point out a contradiction, the speaker must show how it is not a contradiction. Sometimes a team's purpose is unclear. The best strategy is just to answer the question. Many times teams will try to evade the question because they do not know the purpose behind the question. It is best to answer the question and deal with what the other team does with the response at the appropriate time. Sometimes a team will *drop* (a debater's term for never responding to a particular point in a debate) a question and an answer altogether.

The second part of the trick is keeping on track. Speakers must maintain control of their own speech. Consequently, once a question is answered, the best thing to do is go back to the point that was originally being made. Practice will enable the debater to use the answer to a question to lead into the next argument. Though not all segues are or can be neat, the least the speaker can say is, "Now, back to the point I was making."

Primarily speakers must remember that they control the platform and can choose to put off an answer until a later part of the speech. The speaker can address the question by saying, "I will respond to that question later when I get to the off case" or "I'll address that very point in the next argument." Allowing the opposing team to control the content of the speech diminishes the power of the speaker. If the opposing team is taking a long time making a point, cut the team off or ask the speaker to get to the point. When the opposing team asks a question, it takes away from the speaker's time. Consequently, the speaker should take questions judiciously. Usually two to three questions per constructive speech is sufficient. Avoiding questions altogether usually makes the speaker look timid and afraid of questions, but accepting all of the opposing team's questions can make the speaker look weak and out of control. Speakers should also remember that if they fail to take questions, the opposing team may fail to address the speaker's questions when the opposing team has the floor.

Answering questions is an acquired art. Time and practice will enable debaters to learn to enjoy and use points of information to their advantage.

Similar to the point of information is the heckle. **Heckling** can have the same effect as a point of information, but without the same formality. Heckles should be short, witty comments the opposing team offers while seated. They should respond to the subject currently being addressed on the floor, and they should advance the case of the team offering the heckle. Heckles should not be intrusive to the speaker, nor should a heckle be rude. Some judges encourage the use of heckles; others disapprove of them. Asking the judge before the round will allow you to make the most of the opportunity to use the heckle.

POINTS OF ORDER

Points of order are really questions of procedure addressed to the judge rather than to the opposing team. Points of order ensure that the rules of procedure are being followed and that the debate evolves in as fair a manner as possible. The original set of guidelines included in the National Parliamentary Debate Association Constitution lists four possible uses of the point of order: when a new argument is introduced in rebuttal, when a speaker carries a pen to the lectern or places his or her hands in his or her pockets, when the speaker goes beyond the time limit, or when prepared material has been brought into the debate. The first and last reasons listed here are the most common and the ones that will be expounded on in this section.

The primary reason for a point of order to be raised is to object when a speaker advances a new argument in rebuttal. Rebuttals should be used to summarize the arguments presented during the constructive period. Speakers should refrain from launching into new attacks during the rebuttal period. This is especially critical for the Prime Minister, since the Opposition will have no opportunity to respond to any new arguments raised during the Prime Minister's speech.

Sometimes it is difficult to determine whether an argument is new or not. This is a primary purpose of the point of order. Let us examine two examples to make the distinction clear. Suppose a Government team argued in the constructive period that welfare mothers milk the system by having more babies to get larger welfare payments. In rebuttal, the Government argues that welfare mothers must care for their large families and therefore the system of health care should be modified to care for the growing number of families on welfare. Although there is a common denominator in the welfare families, the argument is not the same. Consequently, the argument is not permitted in rebuttal. Conversely, the Opposition could take that same argument about welfare mothers milking the system and argue that people do not have children to obtain an extra couple of hundred dollars a month. The Government could come back in rebuttal and argue that when you are living at poverty level, even a few dollars makes a huge difference in how the whole family lives. In this case, the argument is an extension of a previous argument and is also a direct response to an

Opposition argument. Judges will generally give the Prime Minister a fair range of latitude in responding to the Opposition block during the Prime Minister rebuttal. Since the Opposition has twelve minutes of uninterrupted speech, the prime minister can generally respond in new ways to new arguments that have been brought up in the Member of Opposition constructive. The Leader of the Opposition must be careful not to raise new arguments in rebuttal. The Leader of the Opposition can only summarize the arguments and not expand on arguments brought up in the Member of Opposition constructive.

The other time that the point of order is used is when specific knowledge is brought into the debate. Parliamentary debate has evolved in such a way to prohibit the use of prepared material during the debate. But prepared material can often come in the form of specific knowledge. If a team were to cite specific statistics on government spending, for example, the opposing team could rise to a point of order, claiming that this was specific knowledge. Specific knowledge is a challenge in parliamentary debate. Without prepared materials, a debater cannot prove that the statistics being cited are accurate. Contrarily, the opposing team cannot prove that the statistics are not accurate without prepared evidence. When specific knowledge is used, the debate becomes a battle of we said/they said. The judge's particular knowledge and bias can therefore play an unfair role in the outcome of such debates. Debaters should rely on common knowledge to produce the fairest debates.

Form

If such an infraction occurs, the opposing team may rise to a point of order. To do this, the speaker stands, with hand on head and other arm outstretched, and announces "Point of order." The judge will stop the clock and acknowledge the point. The person should state the point as succinctly as possible and then sit down. In the case of a new argument, the person raising the point would say, "Point of order: This is a new argument. Though the issue of welfare mothers has been raised, advocating a reform of the health care system is a new argument."

The person who holds the floor cannot make an argument as to the validity of the point. The Speaker of the House will make a judgment by saying, "Point well taken," "Point not well taken," or "I'll take the point under consideration." When the Speaker of the House finds the point of order is valid and states that the point is well taken, the person holding the floor must stop that line of argument and move on to the next point. If the speaker finds the point invalid and says so, the person holding the floor may continue with the point. If the Speaker of the House takes the point under consideration, the person holding the floor may continue with the point, but the judge may find after hearing the whole argument that the point was out of order. In this case, the judge will ignore the point in later deliberations.

Both teams should try to mask their reactions to these points. Rarely is the judge's reaction indicative of the way the case is going in general. More often than not, the judge rules on that point alone. In any case, one point will usually not make or break a case in parliamentary debate.

The claim of specific knowledge is used less frequently than before in parliamentary debate, but when there is an obviously unfair use of specific knowledge, the opposing team should point out this fact. Points of order about specific knowledge can be raised at any point in the debate, not just during rebuttals. As is the case with new arguments, the person raising the objection should state the case briefly and explain why the specific knowledge is damning. For example, "Point of order: This is specific knowledge. Without the actual cited material, we have no way of testing the validity of the poll that the opposing team is citing."

Rarely do points of order make or break a case, although they can provide a psychological advantage to the team that wins the point. Teams should be careful to use points of order judiciously. Raising more than one or two points of order during a four- or five-minute rebuttal is considered intrusive. If a team is continually raising new arguments, it is better to wait until three or four have been presented and raise a point of order stating, "This whole speech has been a new argument." Even if the point is denied, the opposing team will have raised the objection.

POINTS OF PERSONAL PRIVILEGE

Though rarely used, **points of personal privilege** are permitted in parliamentary debate, usually to refer to conditions of the room and the debate. Conditions of the room include requesting that a door be closed or a window be opened. A more frequently used version of the point of personal privilege is to point out an *ad hominem* attack. Since parliamentary debate believes in the fundamental fairness and civility of debate, *ad hominem* attacks, which attack the person rather than the argument, can be called to the judge's attention.

Points of personal privilege are used infrequently in competition. However, they provide a sometimes useful tool for creating a comfortable debating atmosphere, both physically and emotionally.

CONCLUSION

Points of information, order, and personal privilege are tools that the savvy parliamentary debater will use to advantage. Effective use of these tools enables a team to remain active in the debate even when the other team is speaking. In addition, the use of these points allows the judge to examine how each team controls the tempo of the debate. Points of information and order are among the elements that make the interactivity of parliamentary debate fun and exciting.

Chapter Eighteen

Wit and Humor

One of the elements of parliamentary debate that makes this debate form accessible to the public is the use of wit and humor. When parliamentary debate was first introduced to the western United States, many topics led to frivolous debate. In the ensuing years, topics and debates have come along way to providing more substance for both the debaters and their audiences. There is a fine line between frivolous debates and humor used as a rhetorical tool. We advocate the use of wit and humor to make points, garner attention, and make debates more lively. Hence we borrow Knapp and Porrovecchio's schema of nine practical considerations for the use of humor in parliamentary debate as found in *The Southern Journal of Forensics*. The acronym WITTICISM should be an easy prompt to put the appropriate use of wit and humor into practice.

Wordplay. Wordplay can be one of the easiest ways to inject humor into debates. By using puns, alliteration, and exaggeration, the speaker can not only call attention to arguments but also add rhetorical flourishes that are bound to boost speaker points a fraction or two.

Incongruity. Incongruity allows the speaker to point out inconsistencies in the opponent's arguments while calling special attention to the incongruity by the emphasis naturally added by laughter.

Tone. The manner in which a humorous remark is made can often make the difference between eliciting laughter or sneers from the judge. Tone enables the speaker to impart goodwill in the use of humor.

Timing. No matter what form of humor is used, the speaker should be cautious that the humor is appropriate in the particular context.

Insights. Speakers should remember that humor is an effective way of providing a new perspective on a situation or argument. By casting an argument in a humorous light, the speaker can not only offer a heretofore unexplored insight but also invite the judge to see things from that perspective.

Complicity. The whole of humor is based on the hearer's understanding of the joke. In that regard, making a judge laugh means that the judge is seeing the argument from your perspective.

Injection. Adding humor to parliamentary speeches can often inject life into a dry debate. By doing so, the speaker adds rhetorical flourishes that will add to the judge's assessment of the speaker's rhetorical skill.

Simplicity. Regardless of the comic device used to gain attention, the humor must be self-evident. (If you have to explain the joke, the humor is lost.) In addition, a long or complicated joke may take too much time from a timed speech and not be worth the potential payoff.

Manners. This is perhaps the most important aspect to remember in using humor. Jokes may make fun of arguments but should never make fun of people. *Ad hominem* jokes are rarely funny and almost always damaging to the deliverer's credibility.

These nine directives provide justification, method, and stylistic suggestions for using humor in parliamentary debate.

CONCLUSION

Perhaps the most important thing to remember about using humor in debates is that you must use it for a purpose. Otherwise, debates devolve into fruitless exercises of minimal educational value. However, when used as a rhetorical tool, humor can do more than just add speaker points; humor has the power to persuade.

Chapter Nineteen

Audience Analysis

Key Concept

Audience analysis—the process of discovering attitudes, beliefs, and values of viewers of the debate

---

At a local restaurant one evening, a new staff person, Jerome, was put in charge of our table. Jerome recited the very complicated specials without faltering. He displayed a thorough knowledge of the preparation of the dishes, the wine offerings, and the dessert selections. Clearly, Jerome had studied the menu, learned about the restaurant, and mastered the art of taking diners' orders. Yet when it came time to leave the tip, our party unanimously agreed that Jerome barely deserved the minimum. Why?

Despite his professional thoroughness, Jerome had failed to notice that the elderly member of our party was having difficulty hearing him speak.; he had to be reminded repeatedly to speak up. He also had to be asked several times to bring a baby chair. He recommended steak to the party who asked about vegetarian dishes. We could go on, but the point is clear: Jerome had failed to recognize that we were unique individuals with distinct wants and needs to which

141

he would be wise to cater. In other words, Jerome had overlooked the importance of **audience analysis**.

As a debater, it is essential that you pay close attention to your audience. At
every stage of the parliamentary debate process, you should be considering the
decision maker's perspective. After all, just as Jerome should have realized,
every audience is unique.

In this chapter, we will cover some of the basics of audience analysis in parliamentary debate. We divide it up into three parts: before the tournament, during the tournament, and after the tournament.

BEFORE THE TOURNAMENT

There is a great deal you can do in terms of audience analysis prior to the tournament. Start by considering the geographical location of the tournament.
Follow this with research into recent issues of importance to the state, city, and
the host institution. Get newspapers from the region. See if there are any other
publications focusing on the state, city, and school. What are the "hot" topics?
What regional issues are people talking about?

Following this, find out from the tournament host which colleges and universities will have debate teams competing. With this knowledge, you will
more than likely have an idea of some of the judges you will encounter. Have
you debated in front of any of these people before? Do you have old ballots with
their critiques? Do your teammates have any insights to share? Does your
coach? Taking the time to contemplate the judging pool prior to the tournament
can save you valuable time and effort in the long run.

Once you have completed the initial research, scan the press for the popular
attitudes concerning significant current events. Most likely you cannot anticipate all of the judges you will meet at the tournament, so part of your audience
analysis should consist of gauging popular attitudes on important controversies. What have you read about public attitudes on the topics you believe will
be debated at the tournament? What are the Republicans saying? How about
the Democrats? The media pundits and editorial writers? What about the polls?
Your friends? Your professors? Try to come away from your research with an
understanding of the different perceptions and attitudes of the culture on the
current controversies. This is far from an exact science, but it might help you in
your quest to understand the perspective of your audience.

DURING THE TOURNAMENT

You have completed the pretournament audience analysis research and now find yourself staring at the debate pairings at the tournament. Apart from finding out the room in which you will be debating and who your opponents will be, be sure to write down the judge's name and school code. Find out who your judge is and the institution he or she is affiliated with. Depending on the rules of the specific tournament, you may or may not be able to speak to your coach or teammates to get information about the judge. Perhaps your pretournament research will be applicable here. Ideally, you will know a bit about the individual judging paradigm of the individual. (A *paradigm* is a general model or worldview that guides the decisionmaker.) If you do not recognize the name, look to the institution. In what geographical region is the school located? Is it a private or public institution? Does it have a religious or military affiliation? Do you know it as a more liberal or conservative institution or area of the country? Remember, these questions can only lead you to probabilities. They are far from foolproof.

Your next bit of audience analysis takes place in the debating chambers. Take a good look at your judge. Because you are a human being, you will automatically take in a great deal of demographic information and make inferences about this person. Again, do not jump to conclusions. Make inferences in the full awareness that they are simply best guesses. Although ample room for errors remains, this sizing-up exercise can prove worthwhile. In addition to age, race, and gender, we suggest that you look at other factors for clues. What do you notice about the person's clothing? Is the person wearing or carrying anything distinguishing that might provide insight? A shirt with a message? A *Star Trek* tie? An expensive briefcase? A button on a backpack? Can you guess the person's socioeconomic status? What can you tell about the person's manner? Does it seem very formal? Informal? Does the person seem to assume substantial power over you or treat you as an equal? Again, the best you can do is make educated guesses. Avoid forcing the issue. If you cannot get a good read on someone based on manner and clothing, you may find the person more revealing during the debate.

Some judges try to mask their responses to the arguments in a debate; others are quite expressive. For example, in a final debate with three judges, the Government team began the first constructive speech speaking very rapidly. After about two minutes, two of the judges had dropped their pens and were shaking their heads in disgust. Unfortunately for the Government team, the speaker never made the effort to notice. Had she simply glanced up and evaluated the situation, she could have adjusted her delivery to fit the judges' paradigms.

Remember, audience analysis continues throughout the rhetorical situation. This means that during the debate, you should be very aware of the nonverbal communication of your judge. Look at the reactions the judge makes to arguments brought up by both sides. Is it apparent which arguments are successful? Sometimes it will be. This ongoing analysis becomes crucial as you prepare your rebuttal speech. Remember, the rebuttal speeches should serve to crystallize the debate down to the significant issues. You might just be able to gather which issues seem most salient in your judge's mind by the nonverbal displays.

AFTER THE TOURNAMENT

Audience analysis should not end with the tournament. Many matters require continuing thought. What do the ballots say? Did the judges reveal something about themselves that might prove important next time? Do the ballots provide insight into the judge's paradigm? What seemed to be the significant issues for the judge? Did the judge find something particularly compelling? Did he or she seem to pay attention to arguments or delivery? Were points of information cited?

In addition to reading the ballot, some judges will be happy to speak with you after the tournament, especially once the results have been made public. We strongly encourage you to avoid challenging a judge or putting a judge on the spot by demanding an explanation. However, if you find an opportune moment to ask for advice or suggestions for next time, most judges will gladly share their thoughts with you. This information will almost certainly come in handy at a future date.

CONCLUSION

Audience analysis can make the difference between success and failure. You might have a compelling case with logical arguments and a powerful, impassioned delivery yet find yourself in a secondary position because your case contradicts your judge's paradigm. Although most judges attempt to check their biases, there is no such thing as an objective decision. If your judge objects to heckling and considers it rude, you might be docked enough points to lose the debate if you heckle. Audience analysis might help you to avoid such frustrations.

Chapter Twenty

Ethics

Key Concepts

Canned Cases—using previously developed cases in parliamentary debate
Ethics—questions of morals in human conduct

- You are debating an inexperienced opponent who appears overwhelmed and frustrated. Do you continually rise for points of information to increase the pressure on him?
- You know the debate judge is a staunch environmentalist. Do you create a case that obviously reinforces her views?
- Your partner builds a compelling case that necessitates withholding information broadcast that morning. Do you go ahead with the case and withhold the new information?

As a speaker engaged in public argument, you will inevitably find yourself confronting questions of right and wrong. Although you may not encounter the specific situations just described, chances are you will face complex issues requiring you to make deliberate decisions concerning principled communication.

The *Oxford English Dictionary* defines *ethics* as "moral principles; rules of conduct." The study of ethics focuses on questions of morals in human conduct. The term *moral* often concerns notions of good and bad, right and wrong, appropriate and inappropriate. Most colleges and universities offer courses in ethics that span many disciplines.

In this chapter, our focus will be on ethics and debate. Our purpose here is not to define what should or should not be considered ethical behavior; rather it is to draw attention to some of the situations you might find yourself in as you engage in public argument and debate. It is our hope that consideration of such issues before they arise will assist you in producing a debate ethic based on reflection and forethought rather than expediency and convenience.

All communication encounters have ethical dimensions. From conversations with your friends to spats with your romantic partner to discussions with colleagues and authority figures, you no doubt confront questions of morality and appropriateness on a daily basis. Although there is no ethical road map for public argument and debate, a consideration of common situations may assist you in creating a framework for your own decision making. We encourage students and educators to discuss their philosophies concerning the dilemmas presented in this chapter.

PREPARED VERSUS CANNED CASES

Since parliamentary debate is an extemporaneous debate format, you have little time in which to prepare arguments and cases. However, as you gain experience, you will find that certain subjects and issues come up quite regularly. Furthermore, the abstract nature of many resolutions lends itself to a wide range of interpretation by participants. Inevitably, debaters find themselves in situations in which they can adapt a case or thesis they have debated previously to fit the parameters of the current proposition before the House.

For example, if you and your partner successfully supported the resolution *This House supports same-sex marriages* and a short time later faced a different team with the resolution *This House would subvert the dominant paradigm*, is it ethical for you and your partner to reuse the successful case idea concerning same-sex marriages for your debate on subverting the dominant paradigm? As with all controversies, there are strong arguments for different positions.

Nothing formally prohibits the employment of previously used cases in parliamentary debate, and banning such a practice would be problematic, if not impossible, to enforce. Proponents of the practice of recycling case ideas argue that debaters who go to the effort of refining cases and strengthening the lines of argument should be rewarded for their hard work. Likewise, advocates of this position claim that Opposition teams maintain the advantageous side from the outset since it is generally easier to tear down a case than to build one up. The practice of preparation is viewed as essential for advocates to remain competitive.

Finally, proponents argue that such preparation is inevitable since experienced debaters will naturally gravitate toward cases and arguments that have proven successful in past debates.

Opponents of this practice claim that such "canned" cases represent an unethical practice in parliamentary debate since they violate the very nature of this extemporaneous debate practice. These critics claim that the fifteen to twenty minutes of preparation common to parliamentary debate should be adhered to by both teams. In fact, opponents argue, the debate actually begins once the resolution has been read, and the preparation time is part of the debate. These critics assert that canned cases undermine the very nature of the activity and produce an unfair advantage for practitioners.

USE OF PREPARED MATERIALS

Another area of ethical consideration for parliamentary debaters concerns the use of evidence. As we prepare to publish this book, written evidence is prohibited from the debating chambers in competitive parliamentary debate. This means that debaters may consult published materials during the preparation time but may not bring those materials into the debating chamber. This has created quite a bit of confusion and controversy among coaches and competitors. Understandably, questions concerning plagiarism and the ethical guidelines respecting evidence are of concern to all participants.

Plagiarism refers to the practice of taking and using another person's thoughts, writings, and inventions and passing them off as one's own (OED 1138). This definition comes from the *Oxford English Dictionary;* if I failed to divulge that fact, I might be guilty of plagiarism. Public argument and parliamentary debate in particular present a challenge for debaters wishing to make powerful arguments while avoiding theft of another person's thoughts and ideas.

Standards for plagiarism depend on the context in which communication takes place. If you are conversing with a friend and repeat statistics on downsizing from an article you read in the *Wall Street Journal*, you would not be guilty of plagiarism if you failed to cite the author and the exact date and place of publication. However, if you repeated the same statistics in a public forum you would have to give credit to your sources of information.

The National Parliamentary Debate Association advises debaters to consider a *common knowledge* standard for their argumentation. As stated previously, common knowledge is defined loosely as "what a college undergraduate should be familiar with." This necessarily ambiguous definition results in controversy when debaters claim that cases or lines of argumentation violate the common knowledge guideline and represent specific knowledge. As a debater, you must make deliberate choices as to the appropriateness of supporting material you employ for your arguments. So what is a debater to do?

A norm that many people agree to asks debaters to explain, clearly and accurately, all examples or evidence that may be unfamiliar to their opponents. It is unlikely that anyone would base an entire case on specific knowledge, but debaters should be expected to explain examples or evidence they cite to support their claims.

For example, if a debater puts forth the argument that school uniforms in seventh through twelfth grade may prevent violent confrontations based on gang affiliation and subsequently cites an example of the experience she had with her own high school education, she would need to recount the situation fully and accurately and to respond openly and honestly to all points of information from her opponents. Although her opponents might not be familiar with the circumstances surrounding her specific example, they could certainly present counterarguments and examples attacking the evidence and the claim as presented. Questions concerning such issues as enforcement of the policy, follow-up, other factors leading to a reduction in violence, impact on morale, and a host of other questions and lines of refutation would be available and appropriate. Most audiences would expect the nationwide controversy surrounding school uniform policies to be common knowledge so that debaters unfamiliar with one specific case could argue intelligently at a more generalized level. We expect this area to remain controversial and expect that proposals for change will continue to arise.

INTERPERSONAL BEHAVIOR

Still another area of ethical consideration for debaters is the interpersonal behavior of participants. Is it ethical for you to heckle an inexperienced and clearly intimidated opponent? At what point does an attempted display of wit become an offensive remark? How about your tone of voice and volume when you are speaking? At what point might it be labeled rude and perhaps offensive? What about language choices? When does an argument become a personal attack?

Parliamentary debaters enjoy the option of calling a point of personal privilege when they believe they have been the recipient of a personal attack. If you believe your opponent has attacked you personally, you rise for a point of personal privilege and the judge will rule on whether the comments merit sanctioning. In most formats of public debate, a moderator, or perhaps the organizers of the debate, might be the recipients of appeals by debaters claiming *ad hominem* attacks. Ultimately, however, it will be the audience who will decide if and when an arguer has overstepped the boundary. Indeed, often the most effective sanctioning results from the reactions of audience members who generally expect debaters to focus their comments on the issues at hand and to avoid personal attacks. Definitions of rudeness and offensive behavior vary greatly among people and you cannot be expected to know everyone's individual standard. However, that is no excuse for belligerence and inattention to one's own responsibility as an ethical communicator. Our advice would be to err on the side of caution rather than risk the loss of credibility that comes from insulting behavior.

As should be evident from the foregoing discussion, ethical argumentation requires maturity and sound judgment. There is nothing simple about listening to another person challenge your ideas. It is especially difficult if you perceive that person to be doing so in an especially aggressive and disrespectful manner. Yet resorting to similar behavior will most likely lead to a severe reduction in your own credibility and do nothing but create a backlash and an escalation of unproductive conflict.

CONCLUSION

The clash of ideas can produce an exciting, dynamic and ultimately constructive intellectual exchange. With honest, open, and mutually respectful argumentation and debate, audiences and participants can benefit enormously.

Part IV

Elements of Competitive Debate

Chapter Twenty-One

A Brief History of Parliamentary Debate in North America

Before participating in competitive parliamentary debate, it may be helpful to understand the origins of parliamentary debate in the western United States. In addition, knowing this history will help you to recognize the names and conventions of this form.

At the writing of the text, there are three recognized parliamentary debate associations in North America: the National Parliamentary Debate Association (NPDA), the American Parliamentary Debate Association (APDA), and the Canadian University Student Intercollegiate Debate Organization (CUSID). All three associations practice various forms of parliamentary debate on the national and international level. Like most historical accounts, the histories of these organizations are debatable, subjective, and incomplete.

It is generally understood that CUSID was the first academic debate organization in North America formed to foster competitive parliamentary debate. Although students may have been debating in a parliamentary style for years, CUSID was officially formed in the mid-1970s. CUSID formation followed the creation of the Trans-Atlantic University Speech Association (TAUSA), which attempted to bring together debaters from Great Britain, Canada, and the United States. To participate in TAUSA, Canadian debaters formed CUSID and sent teams to London in 1976 for international competition. CUSID has thrived in a more or less consistent format since its inception. Today the organization boasts hundreds of members representing more than thirty institutions of higher learning.

On the East Coast of the United States, students at Ivy League colleges had been participating in parliamentary-type debates for years before APDA was formed. Both APDA and CUSID are student-run organizations. Although some member institutions may receive financial assistance from their respective administrations, the constitution, governance, and organization of these entities are all products of student effort and oversight. APDA has more than fifty member institutions; it sponsors a national tournament and fields numerous teams at the annual World Parliamentary Debating Championships.

NPDA is unique in that it is the only faculty-sponsored parliamentary debating association in North America and, indeed, most of the world. As part of forensics programs at member institutions, NPDA students compete under the guidance of college and university professors, and graduate students act as coaches and adjudicators. At the time of this writing, NPDA is the largest parliamentary debating organization in the world, with more than 120 member institutions both public and private throughout the United States.

CONCLUSION

Knowing the history of competitive parliamentary debate in North America will enable you to appreciate the immense popularity of the activity. In addition, you can recognize the universal nature of parliamentary debate. You are not alone!

Chapter Twenty-Two

The Parliamentary Experience

When most people think of competitive debate, they often think of the actual round when the speakers and their ideas clash. Yet the debate experience is really an ongoing process that begins well before the tournament starts and ends long after the last trophy is presented. In this chapter, we hope to describe briefly what eight days in the life of a debater are like. Keep in mind that the exercises outlined here will vary from team to team and person to person, depending on the goals of both. You may end up putting in many more hours than described here. Preparation for the national championships will be more intense than for a parliamentary warm-up tournament. Nonetheless, this should just give you an idea of what to expect.

MONDAY

Assume that we had no tournament the weekend prior to this Monday. Monday will be spent researching. Depending on the team, that may mean working on the extemporaneous file,[1] completing information logs, or just plain reading—or all three, since the parliamentary debater must be well versed in a variety of top-

---

[1] Extemporaneous is an individual event that requires students to answer a question about current affairs. Students have one half-hour to consult a file of information to construct their seven-minute speech. Students prepare for extemporaneous by preparing a file that compiles information from a variety of news sources.

ics. While the extemporaneous file keeps the debater up to date on current events, information logs provide a broad base of knowledge in areas not necessarily related to current happenings. Information logs provide historical background and context on subjects such as affirmative action, natural rights, and Marxism, as do readings of literature, history, philosophy, and political theory.

Whatever the form of research, you can rest assured that the more you do, the better a debater you will be (and a generally well rounded human being). It is difficult to quantify how much time you should devote to research, but you can probably never do too much. One of the beauties of competing in parliamentary debate is the information that you learn in your other classes doubles as debate research since many of the theories and historical facts can be used in a round at some time.

TUESDAY

On Tuesday, you will be involved in a team case discussion. A case discussion centers on topics or resolutions that the team thinks are likely to come up at a tournament. You will see as you progress in parliamentary debate that even though identical resolutions are rare, the same general issues recur quite frequently. For example, one weekend you might get the resolution *This House would ban the death penalty*. The next weekend you might come across the topic *This House believes in an eye for an eye*. While the second resolution could be interpreted in a variety of ways, it can clearly be connected to the issue of capital punishment. Consequently, the more you talk about broad issues like freedom of the press, environment, human rights, and the right to privacy, the better prepared you will be when specific resolutions are related to these broad issues.

A case discussion will mean talking about the issues from competing sides of the case. Case discussions will occur when each person on the team has done research on the topic so that the discussion is an *informed* discussion. The team will discuss possible ways to structure the case, examples that might be used to support the arguments, and values that might be the best to uphold given the topic.

Case discussions can occur with an entire team, just with your partner, or anywhere in between. Case discussions differ from practice debates in that a debate requires that you stick to one approach and live or die by that approach. Case discussions tread through the possibilities before you have to commit to one approach. In addition, they allow you to consider possible attacks on that position so that you can prepare for those attacks in the Government role. In the Opposition role, these attacks may come in handy if you compete against a Government team that uses one of these approaches.

A case discussion is an extended version of what occurs during preparation time. If you have had the extended version of the case discussion, prep time will be a lot easier since you will already have done much of the work. Further, though you may not have discussed the exact resolution or issue, a case discussion that is similar will often lead you to an appropriate approach because the issues are similar. Often just the process of discovering relevant issues and plans can become a formula or habit that will kick in when the actual tournament arrives.

WEDNESDAY

Finally, the time has come for a practice debate (or two). Obviously, the more practice debates you do, the better off you will be. Profitable practice debates are those that resemble debates in tournaments. Government and Opposition teams are assigned, and you should debate with your regular partner to promote an understanding of how each of you thinks and debates. The round can be adjudicated by a coach or by fellow competitors. We like to have competitors judge to foster a better appreciation of the judge's perspective.

After the practice round, the person adjudicating will tell who won and why. Then you will discuss what happened and evaluate both case and performance. Remember that parliamentary debate is about both content and style. Practice rounds should be about perfecting both sides of the formula. In evaluating both, we will note both the positive and the negative, what went well in the round, and what went poorly. When we consider the case, did the position work? Were there weaknesses that could have been taken care of by the speakers? How did the Opposition attack the case? Were there errors that the Opposition failed to catch? Did the value work? These are just some questions that can be asked to evaluate the content of the debate.

Practice rounds are essential for not only getting experience but also preparing for a tournament round with similar subject matter. So the more rounds that you can do with all kinds of topics, abstract and straight, fact, value, and policy, the better off you will be.

THURSDAY

More research and practice debates are in the offing. A lot may have happened since Monday, so keep up with current events. Thursdays are often travel days to tournaments, so you can do some reading in the van. If you have the opportunity, completing another practice debate, in addition to conferring all the usual benefits, will get you in tournament mode.

FRIDAY AND SATURDAY

Tournament day! Tournaments are usually interspersed with individual events, so the six preliminary rounds of parliamentary debate will usually be spread out over two days. Let us take a look at how one round evolves.

First pairings of who you will debate will be posted on a wall somewhere in the area where everyone gathers. The pairings will list which side you are on and who you are debating against along with the room number and the judge. Some teams keep files on judges to help them anticipate what each tends to look for specifically in a debate. Even those teams will be in the dark regarding hired or new judges. You may want to talk to your coach or teammates about the opposing team or the judge.

Go to your assigned room as soon as possible. Make sure you are there at the time set for the beginning of the round. Once both teams have arrived in the room, the resolution will be read. If you are not there on time, many judges will disqualify you or will read the topic anyway. The rules for the NPDA national tournament state that the Government team has the right to stay in the room and the judge and Opposition must leave. The Government team may choose to leave as well. Both teams have fifteen minutes to prepare. Be forewarned that at least one partner should carry a stopwatch and keep track of preparation

	Signing In on the Board		
Gov	Pitt CM	Opp	Berkeley OS
PM	Ima Cathedral	LO	Cal Oskie
MG	Peter Mitchell	MO	Mario Savio

time so that you can reenter the room with at least thirty seconds remaining. Never be late reentering the room; you can and will be penalized for it.

When you return to the room, you should sign in on the board, listing your school code and the speaker positions and who will speak in those positions. The judge will call the House to order and call on the first speaker. At the end of each speech, the judge will thank the speaker and call on the next speaker. Each speech begins with the Speaker of the House recognizing the various members in the chamber, the judge, the opposing team, and any spectators.

When the round is completed, the teams will shake hands and comment on the fine round and then go back to the gathering area to see the postings for the next round. Generally there are six preliminary rounds during a tournament. Most parliamentary debaters engage in individual events as well as debates and will have other events in which to compete when parliamentary debates are not taking place. If you are just doing parliamentary, you can read, do homework, or engage in round evaluation or case discussions.

SUNDAY

Beginning on Saturday night or on Sunday morning, out rounds or elimination rounds begin. These rounds occur exactly the same way as preliminary rounds. The only exception is the assignment of sides. If the teams in an elimination round did not meet in preliminary rounds, the sides will be determined by a coin flip. If the teams did meet in prelims, the teams will be assigned opposite sides from prelims. There will also be a minimum of three judges in out rounds.

Once the tournament is over or your team is eliminated, ballots from the prelims and out rounds are available to your team. Team philosophies vary about when you will get to see your ballots, since the judges will have written comments and justifications for their decisions on a ballot.

MONDAY

Following a weekend tournament, you will use Monday to evaluate your performance. You can do this by analyzing the ballots. Were there common errors in rounds? Did judges make consistent comments about your speaking style? Were there mistakes that you made that could have been avoided? Were there quirks with a judge you need to remember? All of these issues will help you to improve your debate performance at the next tournament and make you a better speaker and thinker in the long run. Once you have learned what you can from your ballots, do your research. Was a topic introduced that you knew too little about? Look it up now!

CONCLUSION

This is what a typical week looks like. Not every team or competitor will follow this structure, but it should provide a basis for understanding that there is a lot of work that takes place outside of rounds, real or practice. Working with your team and your coach is the best way to figure out parliamentary debate quickly and effectively.

Chapter Twenty-Three

Time/Space Cases

As this book goes to press, the so-called time/space case is out of favor as a Government case strategy in NPDA debate. Still, while the fate of time/space cases remains uncertain, it is worthwhile to understand this Government strategy. We will define the time/space case, provide examples, and outline some tactical advantages and disadvantages you should consider as a parliamentary debater.

In the time/space case, the Government frames the debate by taking it out of the current rhetorical situation and placing it in an alternative historical era as well as changing the identities of those involved in the debate. An example of a time/space case took place at a tournament at Colorado College in 1996. The resolution read something approximating the following: *This House believes that a free press is more important than national security.* The Government team decided that the case of the Unabomber (an anti-technology zealot who at the time of the debate was simply an unknown person or group who had claimed responsibility for terrorist acts in the name of attacking technology) provided a reasonable example of the clash between national security and a free press. The Prime Minister explained in her constructive that a few months ago, the *New York Times* and the *Washington Post* had decided to print the Unabomber's "Manifesto" (a lengthy document submitted by the Unabomber to a few major media outlets) after an extended public debate. She explained in her constructive speech that the editors and journalists at the papers had struggled over whether or not they should print the writings of an avowed terrorist. She claimed that this was an important debate and that it was worth having again. Therefore, the Prime Minister explained that "for the purposes of this debate, the Opposition team will represent those opposing the publication of the manifesto, while we on this side of the aisle shall represent journalists supporting a free press advocating its publication. You, Mr. Speaker, are the editor in chief of the *Times* and the *Post*, and you must make a decision based on our debate." The Prime Minister went on to explain that the debate is taking place before the actual publication of the manifesto.

In effect, the Government team altered the time frame and those involved in the debate process from Colorado College to a meeting room in the media's headquarters. It is important to note that the shift requires all debaters in the round to refrain from using supporting material for their arguments that postdates the new time frame. In other words, anything that had taken place after the actual publication of the manifesto had to remain outside the rhetorical speeches of the debaters. In addition, the judge or Speaker of the House is not to use his or her knowledge of events succeeding the actual publication to evaluate the debate. Therefore, if two days after the publication of the manifesto another newspaper had received a manifesto from a different terrorist demanding its publication under the threat of violence, the judge would need to do his or her best to discount this piece of information.

In an offshoot of the time/space case, some Government teams chose simply to alter either the time or the space, but not necessarily in combination. For example, in a debate on school uniforms, the Government framed the debate by shifting the space by changing the players involved. The Speaker of House was made the principal of a private high school, the Government team was a group of parents advocating school uniforms, and the Opposition consisted of parents opposed to the idea. The Prime Minister did not shift the temporal context of the debate. In this example, all debaters could use arguments and examples from any and all time periods.

In a similar way, some Government teams chose to alter or shift the time or era in which the debate was purportedly taking place. So in a debate on the resolution *This House believes that the U.S. military is its own worst enemy*, the Government shifted the time to 1974, the immediate post-Vietnam era. This strategy of course attempted to put the Opposition in the position of arguing in a historical era wherein antimilitary sentiments in the United States were very high. This leads us to some of the criticisms of the time/space case.

Whereas the Government team setting up the case to argue the merits of publishing the Unabomber manifesto made a convincing case for the utility of such a time/space shift, many Government teams attempted to exploit the time/space strategy by contextualizing the debate in such a way as to put the Opposition in a nearly defenseless position. Accordingly, many judges criticized the entire practice, which has led to its near extinction.

Another criticism of time/space cases has been that it is disingenuous, if not downright presumptuous, for a human being to attempt to inhabit another person's psyche and debate from that perspective. The argument is that it is ridiculous for a collegiate debater, or even a judge in the late twentieth century, to attempt to assume the identity and mindset of someone from a previous generation with a perspective unique to that individual.

Still another criticism of time/space cases is that it is impossible for a judge to pretend to be in a temporal framework that discounts the perspective gained from events since the historical era in which the decision is supposedly being made. In the example of Unabomber debate, is it realistic to believe that the judge would be able to temporarily discount or ignore the events following the actual publication of the Unabomber's manifesto? If publication had in fact assisted the authorities to arrest the Unabomber, would that information not bias the judge's decision in favor of publication?

Several other criticisms have also been raised, but our purpose here is not to refight the debate over time/space cases. However, we do wish to stress that the time/space case is now out of favor and that should its popularity reemerge, you as a debater should keep in mind the criticisms we have mentioned.

If you and your partner should choose to employ a time/space case or an offshoot thereof, we suggest that you spend sufficient time justifying your decision to employ this strategy. The so-called link story that we have referred to previously becomes extremely important. It is vital that the Prime Minister constructive contain a narrative that describes the utility of such an interpretation. The Prime Minister must carefully explain to the judge and debaters on the other side of the aisle why such a time/space shift is justifiable.

CONCLUSION

In this chapter we have discussed the Government strategy known as the time/space case or time/space shift. We have described what it is, presented offshoots and alternative methods for its use, and noted some criticisms put forth by judges and debaters alike. We will refrain from either advocating or discouraging the use of time/space cases. However, we urge you to be familiar with their existence and to keep abreast of the parliamentary debate community's sentiment concerning their legitimacy.

Chapter Twenty-Four

Judging Parliamentary Debate

The judge of an academic debate plays an important role in determining the nature of the activity. The judge is in a position to reward effective argumentative techniques and to discourage the use of poor arguments. The educational quality of academic debate depends upon effective intelligent communication between judge and student. By making fair decisions the judge encourages continued participation in debate.

—Walter Ulrich, *Judging Academic Debate*

There are as many philosophies about judging debate as there are debate judges. This presents a challenge for arguers and bestows on the judge a set of responsibilities and important considerations to keep in mind throughout the debating process. In this chapter, we discuss the debate roles judges fulfill, describe the mechanics of judging parliamentary debate, and present our suggestions for what debate judges might consider when adjudicating rounds. (We use the terms *judge* and *adjudicator* interchangeably.)

At the most elementary level, the judge acts as facilitator and decision-maker for the debate. As facilitator, the debate judge is responsible for clarifying the guidelines for the debate, responding to any questions or controversies that may arise, and helping to create a communication climate that is both constructive and equitable. As a decision maker, a judge must reach and and communicate the decision in a fair, open, and honest manner.

Whatever your particular belief about the nature of debate, should you choose to participate as a judge, your actions and demeanor will have a tremendous bearing on the entire debating process. We hope this chapter provides novice judges with the necessary information to begin adjudicating. A further aim here is to provide experienced judges with meaningful issues for their consideration. Finally, we urge debaters to read this chapter to understand the role of the judge and to consider the significant issues that arise when occupying the judge's chair.

Competition or Education?

We begin with the important controversy surrounding the entire idea of the formalistic judging of debate. Many communication theorists cringe at the idea that public or academic debate demands that judges or audiences choose winners and losers. These critics claim that reducing debate to a contest promotes competitive discourse and unnecessarily pits ideas and people against one another, producing unneeded and unhealthy conflict. Still others view debate as the beneficial and productive clashing of ideas inevitable in a pluralistic democracy. Proponents of this view tend to see formalized debate as educational for both the audience and the debaters involved.

BIAS

Most judges and decision makers attempt to view public debates with an open mind. It would obviously be unfair to render a decision before the debate has even begun. Nevertheless, we must recognize the subjective nature of the adjudication process when considering our approach to judging. Winkler, Newman, and Birdsell (157) point to three primary areas wherein bias tends to surface:

- ❧ Political beliefs
- ❧ Perception of the purposes of debate
- ❧ Beliefs about the role of the judge in debate

We discuss each of these in turn.

Aristotle's observation that we are political animals suggests that we come to debates with experiences, attitudes, and beliefs shaped by a confluence of factors creating our political ideology. By their very nature, debates bring to the forefront controversial and often contentious issues. Consequently it is important to recognize your personal views and attempt to regard the debate not as a referendum on your political beliefs but as a singular event wherein your responsibility is determining which side did the better debating. Likewise, it is important to remember that in many debates the participants did not choose which side of the proposition they would be supporting. If you are incapable of voting against your personal political beliefs, you would do well to remove yourself from the judge's chair.

This leads us directly into the question of your beliefs concerning the purposes of debate and your role as judge. Do you view debate as a laboratory for argumentation and therefore base your decision on what your perceive as the most logically sound arguments and positions? Or do you see debate as more of an exercise in persuasion and communicative ability and render your judgement for the team exhibiting the stronger persuasive appeal? Or perhaps you look for a combination of the two? Regardless of your individual notion of the proper roles of both debate and judges participating in the process, it is useful to acknowledge these assumptions and endeavor to incorporate them into your decision making in a fair, equitable manner. Also, for the benefit of the participants, it is useful to communicate your perspective prior to the actual debate.

PARADIGMS

A judging paradigm is the lens or filter through which you view the debate. The term *paradigm* was made popular by Thomas Kuhn in his 1970 work, *The Structure of Scientific Revolutions*, in which he discussed, among other issues, the impact of the approaches we have to questions and controversies. The particular approach or paradigm of the debate judge will affect how the debate is perceived and evaluated. Hence it is beneficial to become familiar with some of the more frequently employed approaches to judging debate. The following is not meant as an exhaustive discussion of all judging paradigms but as an introduction to common approaches to judging.

Tabula Rasa

The *tabula rasa paradigm* seeks absolute objectivity as its goal. The Latin phrase for "blank slate" metaphorically positions the debate judge as an empty surface or canvas on which the debaters may sketch their ideas and arguments. The *tabula rasa* judge seeks to remove all biases and subjectivity, placing the responsibility for choosing the mechanism for evaluation of the debate round on the shoulders of the participants in the debate. Debaters confronting a *tabula rasa* judge need to state their positions and the impacts of their argumentation explicitly. Avoid making assumptions with a *tabula rasa* judge, and be clear-cut and comprehensive in your argumentation.

Hypothesis Testing

The *hypothesis testing paradigm* places the judge in the position of a scientist evaluating arguments to determine the truth or falsity of the proposition. From this perspective, presumption lies with the Opposition and Negative team or against the resolution. Just as scientists employ the null hypothesis, which assumes that no relationship exists among variables to be tested, the judge would view the resolution as false unless proven true by the Government or Affirmative team in the debate.

Games Theorist

The *games theorist paradigm* influences judges to view debate as a contest in which each side begins with an equal chance of winning. Judges view themselves as referees or umpires seeking above all to be fair. Similar to *tabula rasa*, this approach places debaters in the position of having to explain why certain theoretical issues should be decided one way or another. In other words, it is up to the debaters to contest the proper rules for the game.

Narrative Perspective

The *narrative perspective* views argument as narration or storytelling. Employing this perspective, you would view the debate as a series of competing stories. As judge, you would be asking yourself questions such as "Which side is telling a consistent story?" "Is there consistency in explanations of the motives and deeds of the actors discussed?" "Does the story coincide with what I know to be true?" Since the *narrative perspective* reflects cultural notions of truth, debaters should consider the culture within which the argument takes place.

Some judges will consciously apply one of the aforementioned paradigms and others might do so unconsciously. However, some judges may enlist a combination of two or more of the approaches, and others may simply shift from debate to debate. Be aware that a myriad of judging paradigms exist.

JUDGING PARLIAMENTARY DEBATE

The nature of parliamentary debate necessitates a distinct set of expectations and responsibilities for the adjudicator. Judges trained in alternative formats of debate need to make a significant paradigm shift when entering the House of Parliament. Before discussing the unique aspects of this format for debate and its influence on judging expectations, we present the essentials chronologically.

Judges approaching a parliamentary debate round must be familiar with the basic issues and commands. The adjudicator acts as Speaker of the House and therefore is responsible not only for announcing the resolution and recognizing the members of the House but also for ruling on procedural issues that may significantly affect the outcome of the debate. We address those procedural issues here.

The first responsibility of the adjudicator in parliamentary debate is the reading of the motion. This should be the first opportunity for the debaters to hear the resolution; therefore, the adjudicator should be sure everyone has heard it in full. Since clarity is key, there is no harm in repeating the motion in its entirety until all debaters have it written down completely and accurately.

Following the reading of the resolution for debate, teams typically have fifteen minutes of preparation time until the debate commences. It is customary for the Opposition team to leave the room while the Government team may choose to remain. Quite often, both teams prefer to leave the room to avoid discussion in front of the adjudicator. The teams are responsible for returning to the debating chambers at the end of the fifteen-minute preparation time. Should either team return late, the adjudicator may choose to start the clock for the Prime Minister's seven minute constructive speech.

As Speaker of the House, the adjudicator signals the beginning of the debate by calling the Prime Minister to the podium. Typically, adjudicators do so by announcing, "I call this House to order and recognize the Prime Minister for the first constructive speech on the motion." Once the clock starts for the seven-minute constructive by the Prime Minister, it is the responsibility of the adjudicator to signal that the first minute of the constructive speech has elapsed, indicating that points of information from the opposing team are now permitted (points of information are questions or comments raised by the opposing team during the constructive speeches). Traditionally, adjudicators pound the table once, indicating that one minute has elapsed. The same signal is typically used to indicate when the final minute of the constructive speech has begun and when points of information are no longer permitted. It is also customary to provide time signals during all of the speeches.

Once the Prime Minister's constructive speech has ended, the Speaker typically thanks the Prime Minister and calls the Leader of the Opposition to the podium by announcing, "I thank the Prime Minister and now welcome the Leader of the Opposition for the first constructive for the Opposition." The same procedures indicate opportunities for points of information, time remaining, and the recognition of speakers, during the first four constructive speeches. The first four constructive speeches are labeled as such because the arguers are building (constructing) their respective cases.

Following the final constructive speech by the Member of the Opposition, the adjudicator calls forth the Leader of the Opposition for the final opportunity to speak. It is customary for the adjudicator to remind the speaker that while new examples are permitted, no new arguments or issues may be introduced during rebuttal speeches. "I now call on the Leader of the Opposition for a rebuttal speech not to exceed four minutes, and I'd like to remind the speaker that no new arguments or issues may be brought into the debate."

After the Leader of the Opposition's rebuttal, the adjudicator calls the Prime Minister for the final speech of the debate, a five-minute rebuttal. Although no new arguments or issues are permitted in the Prime Minister's rebuttal, the Prime Minister is permitted to respond to any new arguments brought forth during the final Opposition constructive speech. Let's look at an example for clarification.

In a debate on gun control, the Government advocates mandatory training and testing for individuals desiring to purchase a firearm. In the debate, the Government and Opposition struggle over interpretations of the Second

Amendment, the causes of gun violence in the United States, the Brady Law, and the role of the federal government in regulating such practices. The Member of the Opposition rises for the fourth and final constructive speech. In the speech, she brings up the cost of implementing and enforcing such a proposal, a new line of argumentation in the debate. Following her speech, the Leader of the Opposition rises for his four-minute rebuttal and includes the cost issue in his speech. When the Prime Minister rises for the final rebuttal speech of the debate, she is permitted to address the line of argumentation concerning cost, even though neither she nor her partner had done so in the constructive speeches.

Adjudicators must pay close attention during the Prime Minister's rebuttal, for quite often a decision must be made as to whether the Prime Minister is countering an argument put forth in the Member of Opposition's speech or is in fact bringing a new issue into the debate. Following the Prime Minister's rebuttal, it is customary for the adjudicator to signal that the debate has been completed by announcing, "This House is adjourned."

Adjudicators are responsible also for ruling on points of order during the debate. Points of order are claims that a breach of parliamentary procedure has occurred. The member of the House asserting that a breach has taken place will rise and announce to the adjudicator, "Point of order"; at this point the clock is stopped and the Speaker may ask the claimant to explain the perceived breach. It is at the adjudicator's discretion to ask for a response from the opposing team. Following the explanation, the adjudicator responds orally in one of the three ways:

"Point well taken." This indicates agreement with the claimant that a
   breach has occurred.
"Point not well taken." This indicates disagreement with the claimant.
"Point to be considered." This indicates a desire to delay the ruling, and
   the debate simply continues.

The import of breaches in parliamentary procedure in terms of the decision-making calculus are at the discretion of the adjudicator.

ISSUES FOR CONSIDERATION

The format for parliamentary debate creates certain challenges for participants that adjudicators ought keep in mind. Specifically, the historical framework of the House of Parliament, the limited preparation time, and the nature of the resolution in parliamentary debate are all significant issues for consideration in the decision-making calculus of the adjudicator.

As parliamentary debates take place in a fictional House of Parliament, debaters are expected to act in a manner not injurious to their relationship with their fellow members of the parliamentary body. In theory, although they may oppose the motion in one round, they may need the support of their current opponents for a motion coming to the floor of the House at a future date. Therefore, *ad hominem* attacks (attacking the person rather than the argument) and rudeness are frowned upon, and members may raise a point of personal privilege if they believe that such a breach has occurred. If a debater rises to a point of personal privilege, the judge should stop the clock and listen to the claimant's charge. It is at the discretion of the judge or Speaker to listen to a response from the accused. Judges should indicate their ruling by indicating one of the three aforementioned responses. Adjudicators may use their discretion in deciding whether a breach has indeed taken place and how significant this is to the overall decision making calculus.

Another important consideration for adjudicators is the amount of preparation time debaters have. Typically, debaters are allotted only fifteen minutes of preparation time in which to analyze the resolution, construct a case or countercase, and prepare an overall strategy. For judges accustomed to adjudicating other academic formats for debate wherein teams have months to prepare cases on a resolution, this requires a significant shift in terms of expectations for both teams. Judges would do well to keep in mind that it is considerably easier for someone to refute and tear down an argument than it is to construct and build one up. This is especially significant in terms of expectations of the strength of the Government's case.

A third important consideration for adjudicators of a parliamentary debate round concerns the place of the resolution. Opinions vary on the latitude teams are permitted in their interpretation of the resolution, but adjudicators must consider that parliamentary debate resolutions serve as a starting point for the debate. Teams are permitted to link a case by telling what is known as a "link story" that establishes their interpretation as a legitimate example of the original resolution. For example, if the resolution was *This House would regulate the private sector* and the Government linked it to a case involving higher taxes on corporations doing business overseas, it would be at the judge's discretion whether the Government team illustrated a logical progression of ideas to get from the resolution to the Government's case thesis. If the Opposition accepted the link and debated the case as presented, most judges would confine the decision to the issues raised in the debate. If, however, the Opposition objected to the interpretation and argued against the link story, it would ultimately be the judge's decision to accept it or not. Should the adjudicator conclude that arguments have successfully refuted the link story, it should be a major factor in the overall decision-making calculus. Again, literature concerning judging parliamentary debate is almost nonexistent. We strongly encourage educators to explore this vital issue in the evolution of parliamentary debate in North America.

Significant questions deserving the attention of the parliamentary debating community remain:

- How important is delivery?
- What are legitimate expectations for a Government case?
- What are the Opposition burdens?
- Should adjudicators indicate their perceptions nonverbally and/or verbally?
- Should judges heckle?
- Must the Government advocate a change in the status quo when interpreting a resolution as policy?

In this chapter, we have discussed the different roles judges occupy in the course of a debate, popular judging philosophies, the mechanics of judging a parliamentary debate, and important issues for consideration when adjudicating. Judging debate is simultaneously intellectually challenging and intrinsically rewarding. We urge you to take the time to become involved in the debating process.

UNDERSTANDING THE JUDGE'S DECISION

During most debates, the judge or judges will also flow the debate to make sure they keep track of all the relevant arguments. In addition, the judge will often write comments to themselves about the way in which the debate is conducted by the debaters. After the debate is over or during the debate itself, the judge will fill out the ballot. The ballot tells the tabulation room how to score the debate, and a copy of the ballot will be returned to you after the tournament is completed. The ballot contains pertinent information such as the debate number, the resolution, speakers' scores, who won and lost the debate, the judge's name, and the reasons for the judge's decision.

In any given debate, there are probably three different narratives depicting what occurred in the debate. It is rare that a debater and a judge or the opposing team saw the same things happening in a debate. Consequently, the ballot is a valuable tool for both student and coach in determining how to improve the student's skills. Since the judge's opinion is the one that is recorded, knowing how it was reached is vital to understanding how a team might enhance its skills and its chances at success. Regardless of whether you agree or disagree with a judge's decision, knowing how to interpret the judge's ballot may give you clues as to how that judge thinks and can help you understand how to debate for that judge in the future.

We will look at the two parts of the ballot: speaker rank and rate, and comments. This will enable you to make the best use of the information that judges provide.

SPEAKER RANK AND RATE

At the top of the ballot (see Appendix D), there are boxes for each of the speaker positions. Below the boxes are spaces for the judge to rank the speakers (first through fourth) and to give them a rating (30 to 1, 30 being the best). Both of these provide a relative ranking of how each speaker performed in a particular debate. Speaker points (the rating) are used to determine the overall speaker awards at a tournament. Speaker points and ranks are often independent of the actual outcome of the debate. Theoretically, the combined speaker points of the winning team should be equal to or greater than those of the losing team. Low point wins can occur, but we'll discuss this a bit later.

There is a common misperception that the Prime Minister and Leader of the Opposition have an advantage in gaining greater speaker points and better ranks because they have an extra speech. This, however, is not the case, for it also means that the Prime Minister and Leader of the Opposition have an extra speech to screw up. As such, speaker positions have little to do with a debater's ability to garner top rankings and ratings. These points and ranks are based on the speakers' performance in carrying out their assigned duties.

Interpreting the way a judge assigns ranks and ratings is crucial for understanding how to improve your debating. When you look at the ballot, you should consider the rank and rate together. For example, say your partner received first speaker with 28 points. You were assigned fourth speaker but also received 28 points. Clearly in this case, the judge thought you to be just as good a speaker as your partner. The ranks merely serve as a delineating mechanism. However, if you receive the first rank with 28 points and your partner receives the fourth with 16 points, something went wrong in the debate. Either your skill levels are mismatched, your partner dropped the ball in the debate, or your partner did something that displeased the judge terribly. In any case, if this happens consistently in debates, it should give you, your partner, and your coach reason to reconsider what is happening in rounds.

As these examples illustrate, ranks and rates reflect only what happens in one debate. If you have an off debate and your points reflect it, you should consider what happened in that debate and see what you can do to correct the situation. If your points stay at a consistently low level, then that should tell you that you need to do some serious work to improve your argumentation and delivery skills.

There is a grid below the speaker's names that enables judges to illustrate the strengths and weaknesses of each speaker. You should not expect the points from the grid to add up to the speaker points assigned; that rarely happens. But if you have checks at the high end of every category in every debate except in the organization box, you know where you need to do some work. It is not uncommon for judges to ignore these boxes and instead just write comments. In these cases you will have to sift through their comments to see what you need to work on.

You should be prepared also to take the relative ratings of judges with a grain of salt. Since these ratings are subjective, there is no real way to put an absolute value on a number. One judge may give a score of 28 to all debaters in a particular debate, while another judge watching the same debate may not see a speaker worthy of more than an 18. Some judges will assume that no novice can earn more than 25 speaker points. Another judge may feel that no one should get lower than a 20 unless the speaker has done something offensive. The best way to put ratings in perspective is to look at the points from every debate and see what your average points are. This will probably give you the best indicator of where you are in terms of your skills.

WRITTEN COMMENTS

There are generally three types of comments that a judge will write on a ballot: speaker comments, case comments, and reason for decision. Speaker comments are usually aimed at a particular speaker and enumerate the positives and negatives of that debater's speeches. Case comments usually refer to the way either team has constructed the body of its case. Most judges will conclude their ballot with a specific reason for their vote. Understanding each of these types of comments can often help you to become a better debater.

Speaker comments will generally reflect specific things that a debater does in a debate. For example, a judge might write something like "the Member of the Opposition dropped the MG's Nixon example." This indicates that the judge found this to be a critical line of argumentation that the Member of the Opposition failed to attack. This should clue you in that had the member pursued the line, it would have made the Opposition case stronger. The judge may also make more general comments about a particular speaker. For instance the judge might tell the speaker to work on organization or slow down. Comments such as these will often have a direct correlation to the number of speaker points awarded.

Case comments tell the debaters how the judge saw the debate develop. As stated earlier, it is rare that both teams and the judge view the debate in the exact same way. Consequently, the judge will write about the arguments that he or she thought both teams handled well or ones that did not work or needed development. Comments such as "The Government's claim that Hussein is merely attempting to retain sovereignty was disproven sufficiently by the Opposition" allow the debaters to see which arguments the judge viewed as critical.

The reason for decision tells the debaters the main reason that the judge voted as he or she did. The reason for decision (or RFD, as it is called) will often crystallize the debate into one sentence: "The Government did not uphold their its value," "On balance, the Opposition provided more harms than the Government's advantages." Statements such as these tell what the judge viewed as the critical argument in the debate. These comments can provide insights into how that judge will adjudicate in the future. For example, if the judge comments on the value, a team would be wise to remember to hit on the value whenever that judge judges them.

CONCLUSION

Interpreting the ballot can go a long way in helping teams to improve their skills and their strategies in future debates. Ballots are often the only way that a judge has to communicate knowledge about argumentation to a team. Consequently, ballots are a gold mine for teams if they take the time to analyze the feedback from their judges.

Chapter Twenty-Five

Writing the Parliamentary Debate Proposition

The proposition for debate serves several purposes and therefore is an especially significant element of the debating process. A well-written proposition can make the difference between a confused, unproductive debate and a dynamic clash of ideas. Since you may find yourself in the position of having to craft propositions for public debate, here we offer some guidelines to assist you in the process.

Because parliamentary debate propositions range from quite specific to extremely open-ended, these guidelines simply serve as areas for consideration and do not pretend to be unbreakable laws.

In crafting parliamentary debate propositions, central to your consideration should be the extemporaneous nature of parliamentary debate and its current prohibition on the use of written source material during the debate. These constraints on the participants make specialized in-depth subject areas problematic.

For example, a proposition such as *This House believes that the United States should substantially change its foreign policy stance toward Bhutan* might provide the opportunity for a thought-provoking debate for experts familiar with the policy and its possible ramifications. Nevertheless, most of us would require a tad more than fifteen minutes of preparation time to familiarize ourselves with the issues surrounding this area of controversy.

With this in mind, here are our guidelines for writers of parliamentary debate propositions:

1. *Remain cognizant of the format.* Since parliamentary debate prohibits written source material inside the debating chambers and allots fifteen minutes to prepare a case, avoid obscure subject areas with which most debaters will be unfamiliar. Nobody profits from uninformed arguers trying desperately to hide ignorance of a topic area.

2. *Consider timely issues.* One of the most advantageous elements of public debate, in which the subject for debate changes constantly, is the ability to consider pressing issues of the day. When a particularly significant event or series of events take place, people want to discuss it. Parliamentary debate takes the café discussion one step further by allowing for structured and extended deliberation of the issues in front of an audience. The rapidity of scientific and technological change create excellent opportunities for debaters and audiences to engage in a constructive consideration of the issues. Moreover, a debate format so heavily reliant on the faculty of memory encourages deliberation of contemporary controversies. Still, the timely, extemporaneous nature of this debate format also represents an important limitation. In this mass-mediated culture of "instant analysis," an intellectual diet filled exclusively with headline stories is severely limiting. We recommend a combination of current events and timeless concerns.

3. *Write propositions in single declarative sentences.* To avoid confusion and a divided focus, propositions should have a singular locus of contention. Although parliamentary debate propositions are often very abstract (*This House would lead the way*), incorporation of more than one phrase and a bilateral focus would further reduce the potential for a constructive forty-five-minute debate. Imagine a debate with the proposition *This House would significantly increase the minimum wage and improve water safety.* This would place an enormous burden on the Government team and set out two major topic areas for debate.

Two more reasons to write debate resolutions as declarative sentences are to divide up argumentative ground clearly and to mirror legislatures and other decision-making bodies. Propositions written as questions put the opposition in the unenviable position of not knowing how the Government will respond to the question. This makes preparation time exceedingly difficult. And since parliamentary debate is currently modeled after a legislative body, propositions should mirror the House's debates, using motions with a unilateral focus.

Again, members of the House debating motions need to recognize what they are debating and the ground on which they stand.

Perceptions of appropriate or well-written parliamentary debate resolutions remains in dispute. At the time of this writing, participants disagree on some fundamental issues surrounding the crafting of propositions. One example concerns propositions written in the negative or stating rejections of policies or beliefs, such as *This House would not trade advertising space for money* or *This House rejects authority*. Opponents of negative phrasing complain that it complicates the advocates' problems in presenting cases and needlessly confuses the audience. Proponents claim that it recognizes the reality that we are often called on to argue against ideas and policies. What do you think?

Another area of controversy surrounds the level of specific knowledge propositions require. So the proposition *This House supports a flat tax* would be viewed as demanding a level of specific knowledge of federal, state, and local taxes that most individuals do not have committed to memory. Some educators go as far as asking for the prohibition of policy propositions because they inevitably require specific knowledge that parliamentary debaters generally do not possess. Proponents of more directive and specific policy propositions assert the advantage of a more substantive, focused debate. These educators claim that policy debates need not inevitably come down to dueling statistics and statutes.

CONCLUSION

In this chapter, we have discussed some of the considerations to keep in mind when crafting debate propositions. We have discussed the significance of writing propositions emphasizing the strengths and limitations of public debate with limited preparation time and little access to outside published material. Propositions should be unidirectional, diverse, and reflective of the nature of the debating format. We strongly encourage the authors of debate propositions to take the time and make the effort to craft propositions with the potential for constructive and engaging public debate.

Chapter Twenty-Six

The Future of
Parliamentary Debate

The parliamentary debate format is a dynamic, evolving entity. In this final chapter, we would like to examine some areas that are controversial and polarize activists on many sides. Most controversies center around either form or content. We begin with form.

FORM

There are some advocates who would eliminate the traditional titles and actions that make the parliamentary form unique. Speakers would no longer use formal greetings, would not place a hand on their head, and would lose the right to address the Speaker of the House in points of order. The Speaker's role would be greatly diminished in the actual participation of the debate.

The reasons for these possible changes stem from the idea that these nods to the British tradition are frivolous. Advocates of these changes argue that the formal requirements pay homage to a foreign system and do not foster the uniqueness of American parliamentary debate. In addition, points of order are considered to be an intervention from the judge, since the judge states an opinion during the progress of the debate.

Those on the other side of the controversy suggest that these traditions are precisely what sets parliamentary debate apart from other academic forms of debate. In addition, these practices ensure civility in rounds, something other forms are accused of lacking. Some advocates even argue that the introductions offer students the opportunity to argue from a position that is grander than debating at a tournament since debaters are role-playing in a parliament. In effect, the arguments are contextualized so that a greater perspective is gained. Points of order are seen, by advocates of their continued use, as a countermeasure for only one rebuttal for each team. In this way, debaters can state objections that they may not be able to address in the round.

CONTENT

The most controversial issue facing the National Parliamentary Debate Association at this time is the idea of using sources in preparation time and during the actual debate. Under the proposed plan, debaters would be allowed to consult prepared files, teammates, coaches, or any other source during preparation time.

Advocates of the use of outside sources cite the need for better-informed debaters to produce better debates. They suggest that it is unreasonable to assume that debaters can remember all of the facts necessary to argue a minimum of six different resolutions each tournament. They also counsel that the learning experience will be enhanced when students no longer need to rely solely on their own knowledge to create cases and can draw on the collective knowledge of outside sources, their coaches, and their teammates.

On the other side of the aisle, defenders of the status quo argue that allowing sources of any type in prep hinders the educational experience of the individual debater. They reason that resorting to files, coaches, and teammates takes the burden from the individual debaters to make arguments on their own. Further, students relying on prepared files lose the opportunity to approach cases creatively, thereby losing some of the benefits inherent in parliamentary debate—namely, extemporaneous skills and the lost canon of memory.

CONCLUSION

As of this writing, we cannot predict the outcomes of these controversies. The only thing we can predict about parliamentary debate is that it is unpredictable.

Appendix A

Sample Resolutions

This House believes that developing nations need strong dictatorships.
This House would regulate the private sector.
This House believes that censorship is more dangerous than pornography.
This House rejects grades.
This House should encourage bilingual education.
This House will protect its children from television.
This House fears for our judicial system.
This House supports term limits for Supreme Court justices.
This House advocates proportional representation.
This House supports campaign finance reform.
This House would crack the whip.
This House believes that deception is necessary.
This House would act to stop terrorism.
This House believes it is a conspiracy.
This House would help teenagers.
This House believes that libertarianism is inadequate.
This House would violate sovereignty to protect humanity.
This House would limit free speech to facilitate democracy.
This House believes that mainstream journalism in the United States propagates corporate power.
This House believes that the marketplace of ideas is ruled by the wealthy.
This House supports a six-year presidential term.
This House believes class is more important than race in America.

This House believes that war justifies the restriction of civil liberties.
This House would explode the canon.
This House believes there is serious trouble in the ranks.
This House supports states' rights.
This House believes there are too many lawyers.
This House would privatize it.
This House supports home schooling.
This House believes the media have gone too far.
This House believes health care is a right.
This House would plant the seed.
This House would ban it.
This House would limit it.
This House believes that the old is better than the new.
This House believes that gangsta rap reflects more than it affects.
This House would police the "information superhighway."
This House believes that the Left is right.
This House would shoot the messenger.
This House would vanquish the foe.
This House would reject dogma.
This House is estranged from its youth.
This House believes that the emperor has no clothes.
This House believes that resistance is not futile.
This House no longer loves America.
This House should stay at home.
This House believes that the scales of justice have been tilted.
This House would ride the fence.
This House believes that "freedom from" is better than "freedom to."
This House would use the force.
This House would steal the beggar's tin cup.
This House believes that silence is obscene.
This House would crack the whip.
This House condemns the wolf in sheep's clothing.
This House prefers the mysterious to the obvious.
This House believes that deception is necessary.

Appendix B

Sample Topics for Research

Here we present a list of topics that can serve as the starting point for doing research in parliamentary debate. The list is not exhaustive and should expand as you gain knowledge and experience in parliamentary debate.

affirmative action
allegory of the cave
American dream
antisemitism
apartheid
appeasement
balance of power
Bay of Pigs
Berlin Wall
big government
Bill of Rights
bipartisan
book burning
Brahmin
brain trust
brinkmanship

bully pulpit
categorical imperative
centrist
checks and balances
China lobby
civilian review
civil rights
cold war
communism
conservative
containment
cost/benefit analysis
cost of living
Cultural Revolution
demagogue
democracy

détente
deterrent
diversity
dollar diplomacy
divine rights of man
domino theory
doves and hawks
dustbin of history
elitism
empowerment
entitlement
environmentalism
equal time
ethnic cleansing
executive privilege
family values
fascism
feminism
flat tax
four freedoms
free enterprise
gag rule
genocide
gerrymander
glasnost
glass ceiling
Good Neighbor Policy
grassroots
Great Society
gridlock
hate crimes
hegemony
Hobson's choice
home rule
human rights
ideology
imperial presidency

inflation
infrastructure
iron curtain
isolationism
junta
kitchen debate
law and order
liberal
limited war
mainstream
Malcolm X and the Nation of Islam
mandate
manifest destiny
massive retaliation
McCarthyism
measured response
Medicare
melting pot
Middle America
military-industrial complex
moderate
Monroe Doctrine
most favored nation status
multiculturalism
Munich analogy
natural rights
neoconservatism
Nervous Nellies
New Deal
new economics
New Federalism
New Left
new world order
Nixon Doctrine
nonpartisan
nonviolence
normalization

nuclear proliferation
pacification
paradigm shift
partisan
pax Americana
peaceful coexistence
perestroika
pocket veto
police action
police of the world
politically correct
populism
progressive
proletariat
quality of life
quota
recession
reform
religious perspectives
republican
reverse discrimination
right to know
SALT
scorched earth policy
secular humanism

self-determination
silent majority
social contract theory
sphere of influence
states' rights
strict constructionist
Supreme Court
tax sharing
technocrat
terrorism
third world
totalitarianism
Truman Doctrine
Uncle Sam
underclass
utilitarianism
unilateralism
United Nations
voodoo economics
Watergate
welfare state
Weltanschauung
workfare
World War II
zero-based budgeting

You should also be able to define and use the philosophies of the following:

Aristotle
Plato
Thomas Hobbes
John Locke
Niccolò Machiavelli
Bertrand Russell

Immanuel Kant
Marx/Lenin/Engel
Arthur Schopenhauer
Adam Smith
Jacques Ellul
George Santayana

191

For further readings in argumentation theory, consult the following:

Branham, Robert James. *Debate and Critical Analysis: The Harmony of Conflict.* Hillsdale, N.J.: Erlbaum, 1991.

Epstein, Susan B. "What About Research: How to Be 'Well Read.'" *Parliamentary Debate* (Summer 1996): 3–13.

Freeley, Austin J. *Argumentation and Debate: Critical Thinking for Reasoned Decision Making.* 9th ed. Belmont, Calif.: Wadsworth, 1998.

Inch, Edward S., and Barbara Warnick. *Critical Thinking and Communication: The Use of Reason in Argument.* 3rd ed. Needham Heights, Mass.: Allyn & Bacon, 1998.

Perelman, Chaim, and L. Olbrechts-Tyteca. *The New Rhetoric: A Treatise on Argumentation.* Trans. John Wilkonson and Purcell Weaver. Notre Dame, Ind.: University of Notre Dame Press, 1969.

Pfau, Michael, David A. Thomas, and Walter Ulrich. *Debate and Argument: A Systems Approach to Advocacy.* Glenview, Ill.: Scott, Foresman, 1987.

Rieke, Richard D., and Malcolm O. Sillars. *Argumentation and Critical Decision Making.* 3rd ed. New York: HarperCollins, 1993.

Toulmin, Stephen. *The Uses of Argument.* Cambridge, Mass.: The Harvard University Press, 1958.

Trapp, Robert, and Janice Shuetz, eds. *Perspectives on Argumentation: Essays in Honor of Wayne Brockriede.* Prospect Heights, Ill.: Waveland, 1990.

Ziegelmueller, George W., and Jack Kay. *Argumentation: Inquiry and Advocacy.* 3rd ed. Needham Heights, Mass.: Allyn & Bacon, 1997.

Appendix C

Sample Flow Sheet

This House would pledge allegiance to the flag.

PM	LO	MG	MO
pledge in public schools bar=people believe no reason for patriotism V=civic responsibility C= how to imp cr	PS part of gov = gov restric=gov control Just a symbol, has no/ to do w/ pat Grant	Grant	
I. Flag is imp -symbol of nat -m/w died -civil rights	I. Limits choice to disagree w/ nat symbol gets more respect than people	I. Flag led the way, shows how to be responsible as ind World War II	I. Arbitrary symbol -doesn't foster free thought
II. Teaches a lesson - ab gov -mean - ab respons to nat - public school is part of gov	II. Gives a one sided view of gov - only good -children can't exer free choice b/c peer press	II. Provide emot boost to nat - instills positive attitude toward country -national anthem -kids will study history	II. Children don't u/stand flag so won't disr so why would they exer choice -indoctrination
III. Part of personal responsibility - gov control=no ind respons lib=resp -Locke soc/cont	III. Shouldn't pledge to a flag...rather exer respon to self	III. There are ways to change gov w/o disrespect -vote	III. Vote isn't effective -no proof offered it is
IV. Free Speech - can adv b/c Free speech not issue - not required	Drop		

Appendix D

Sample Ballot

Division_____ Round_____ Room_____ Judge _____

Topic _____

Government_____ Opposition _____

_____ _____   _____ _____
PM   MG   LO   MO
Rank_____   Rank_____   Rank_____   Rank_____
Rate_____   Rate_____   Rate_____   Rate_____

In my opinion the better debating was done by _____ (Gov/Opp)
Representing_____(School)

_____

Judge's Signature_____

Comments:

Works Cited

Ericson, Jon M., James J. Murphy, and Raymond Bud Zeuschner. *The Debater's Guide.* Rev. ed. Carbondale: Southern Illinois University Press, 1987.

Freeley, Austin J. *Argumentation and Debate: Critical Thinking for Reasoned Decision Making.* Belmont, Calif.: Wadsworth, 1996.

Gronbeck, Bruce E., Kathleen German, Douglas Ehninger, and Alan H. Monroe. *Principles of Speech Communication.* 13th brief ed. Reading, Mass.: Addison-Wesley, 1998.

Hall, Kermit J., ed. *The Oxford Companion to the Supreme Court of the United States.* New York: Oxford University Press, 1992.

Hill, Bill, and Richard W. Leeman. *The Art and Practice of Argumentation and Debate.* Mountain View, Calif.: Mayfield, 1997.

Hollihan, Thomas A., and Kevin Baaske. *Arguments and Arguing: The Products and Process of Human Decision Making.* New York: St. Martin's Press, 1994.

Johnson, James "Al." "A Veteran Director of Forensics Looks at the Future of Parliamentary Debate." *Parliamentary Debate* 3 (Fall 1994): 1–4.

Knapp, Trischa, and Mark Porrovecchio. "A Comedy of Errors: The Uses of Wit and Humor in Parliamentary Debate." *Southern Journal of Forensics* 2 (Winter 1998): 281–302.

Kuhn, Thomas S. *The Structure of Scientific Revolutions.* 2nd ed. Chicago, Ill.: University of Chicago Press, 1970.

Pearson, Judy C., and Paul E. Nelson. *Understanding and Sharing: An Introduction to Speech Communication.* 6th ed. Madison, Wis.: Brown and Benchmark Pub., 1994.

Pfau, Michael, David A. Thomas, and Walter Ulrich. *Debate and Argument: A Systems Approach to Advocacy*. Glenview, Ill.: Scott, Foresman, 1993.

Rieke, Richard, and Malcolm O. Sillars. *Argumentation and Critical Decision Making*. 3rd. ed. New York: HarperCollins, 1993.

Trapp, Robert. "Parliamentary Debate." National Parliamentary Debate Association. 8 Feb 1998 <http://www.willamette.edu/cla/rhetoric/debate/npda.html>

Toulmin, Stephen. *The Uses of Argument*. Cambridge, Mass.: The Harvard University Press, 1958.

Winkler, Carol, William Newman, and David Birdsell. *Lines of Argument for Value Debate*. Dubuque, Iowa: Brown & Benchmark, 1993.

Wood, Stephan, and John Midgley. *Prima Facie: A Guide to Value Debate*. 2nd ed. Dubuque, Iowa: Kendall/Hunt, 1989.

Ziegelmueller, George W., and Jack Kay. *Argumentation: Inquiry and Advocacy*. 3rd ed. Needham Heights, Mass.: Allyn & Bacon, 1997.

Glossary

Abstract resolutions—propositions that define the relationship among the terms but not necessarily the specific issue to be debated

Ad hominem **fallacy**—attacking the person rather than the argument

Ad populum **fallacy**—claiming that something is true because popular belief dictates its truth

Ad verecundiam **fallacy**—an appeal to an authority who does not have expertise in the field at issue

Agency—the ability to implement the solution to a problem

Alternative solution—an Opposition strategy where the opposition suggests a different plan

Appeal to ignorance—claiming that something is correct because it has never been proven incorrect

Argument—reasoned decision making

Assignment of burdens—the determination of who must argue what

Audience analysis—the process of discovering attitudes, beliefs, and values of viewers of the debate

Begging the question—asserting the premises as the conclusions to be proven

Blame—the determination of who is at fault

Burden of debatability—a Government responsibility to interpret the resolution so that both Government and Opposition have a fair opportunity to debate

Burden of proof—a Government responsibility to prove the resolution true

Burden of topicality—a Government responsibility to develop a case that is germane to the given resolution

Case—the totality of arguments that a team presents to prove its side

Case statement—a team's basic approach to and interpretation the resolution

Causal reasoning—reasoning that implies that one condition or event is the result of another

Claim—a debatable assertion

Clarify—to reiterate controversial points

Clarity—the clear determination of what is to be debated

Clash—the burden of the opposition to argue against what the Government has proposed

Common knowledge—information that is widely available and known by the average college student

Condense—to reiterate the main points of a case

Constructive speech—a speech used to build a case

Criteria— standards by which a decision is made

Critical listening—listening to evaluate and judge

Crystallize—to limit arguments to the winning points

Cure—the solution to the problem

Current events—issues of economic, political, or social interest that are foremost in the public's mind

Debatability—how the resolution will be debated in terms of fact, value, and/or policy

Deductive reasoning—reasoning that applies a held conclusion to a specific case

Defense of the status quo—an Opposition strategy of arguing in favor of the current system.

Equivocation—altering the meaning of a critical term during the course of the debate

"Even/if" analysis—an approach to a case that dictates that a team can object to the overall case based on procedural rules but cannot still debate the particulars

Evidence—data accepted as true that can be used to prove claims

Examples—evidence in the form of specific cases; examples can be categorical, hypothetical, metaphorical, or analogical

Expert testimony—evidence that draws on authority

Fallacy—reasoning that is faulty

False cause—erroneously attributing the cause of an outcome

False dilemma—reasoning that suggests there are only two possible options when in reality there are more than two options

Flowing—note taking during a debate

Government—the team that must affirm the resolution

Ground—the specific case area that a team must defend

Hasty generalization—generalizing on the basis of inadequate cases

Heckling—witty comments made to the opposing team without benefit of a point of information

Historical analogy—comparison to historical events and situations to predict the outcome of current events or situations

Ill—the problem to be solved

Implicit criteria—generally accepted standards

Inductive reasoning—reasoning that draws a general conclusion by considering specific cases

Information log—a method of filing information for use in debates

Inherency—the requirement to prove that the problem stems from the system in question

Issues—significant questions inherent to the controversy

Key terms—terms that are open to controversy and so need to be defined

Language use—effective word choice

Leader of the Opposition—the first and last speaker for the Opposition team

Link—the connection between the case and the resolution

Listening for understanding—listening to comprehend

Member of Government—the second speaker for the Government team

Member of the Opposition—the second speaker for the Opposition team

Non sequitur—putting forth an irrelevant claim

Nonverbal communication—the use of nonlinguistic messages to create meaning

Off case—independent reasons offered by the Opposition asserting why the resolution should not be adopted

Opposition—the team that must negate the resolution

Opposition philosophy—the approach the Opposition will take toward the resolution and the Government case

Oral delivery—use of the voice to emphasize and impart meaning to words

Organization—the distribution and ordering of arguments

Parallel case—reasoning that asserts that two cases are similar enough to draw conclusions about one case based on the other case

Philosophical and political theories—ideas concerning the nature of reality, truth, knowledge, and politics

Physical delivery—use of the body to impart messages

Point of information—a question or statement addressed to the opposing team that attempts to seek or offer information

Point of order—a question of procedure addressed to the judge

Point of personal privilege—a question addressed to the judge seeking a change in the conditions of the debate

Presumption—the concept that assumes that without significant reason to change, no action should be taken

Prime Minister—the first and last speaker for the Government team

Proposition—a statement that suggests the topic to be debated [also known as a *motion, resolution,* or *topic*]

Psychological noise—distractions from within the person that inhibit effective listening

Reasoning—stated or unstated reasons why a claim should be accepted

Rebuttal—reinforcing arguments

Refutation—attacking directly asserted arguments

Resolutional burdens—the responsibility of each team as defined by the resolution

Resolution origin analysis—discovering who is writing resolutions to prepare for issues that are likely to arise in a debate

Resolutions of fact—propositions that ask the debaters to prove that a particular claim is more true than false

Resolutions of policy—propositions that ask the debaters to develop a plan to solve a particular problem

Resolutions of value—propositions that ask debaters to prove that one value is more important than others in a particular context

Signpost—a phrase or term that indicates the relationship between one concept and another

Sign reasoning—reasoning that draws conclusions from states that are observable in other states

Significance—proof that a problem matters

Slippery slope—the assumption that one step will lead to additional steps that will lead to catastrophe

State, explain, support, conclude—an organizational pattern to develop points within a speech, requiring the speaker to state the claim, explain what the claim means, offer evidence to support the claim, and finally, show the implications of the claim

Statistics—evidence that provides numerical quantification of information

Status quo—the current state of affairs

Straight resolutions—propositions in which the subject to be debated is clearly defined

Straw man fallacy—defeating a position that the opposing team has not put forth as a strong or primary position

Timeless questions—issues that cannot be readily answered and have plagued humans since they began arguing

Time/space case—a case argued and judged from the perspective of a different time and place

Truism—a resolution that is interpreted to prove itself

Vocal variety—changes in rate, pitch, and volume to give meaning to words

Voting issues—the key points in a debate that are pivotal to the outcome

Weighing mechanism—the standards by which the audience evaluates the success of the Government and Opposition cases [also known as *criteria*]

Index